PARTICIPATORY ID
From Exclusion to In

Peter Beresford

First published in Great Britain in 2021 by

Policy Press, an imprint of
Bristol University Press
University of Bristol
1-9 Old Park Hill
Bristol
BS2 8BB
UK
t: +44 (0)117 954 5940
e: bup-info@bristol.ac.uk

Details of international sales and distribution partners are available at
policy.bristoluniversitypress.co.uk

British Library Cataloguing in Publication Data
A catalogue record for this book is available from the British Library

ISBN 978-1-4473-6049-0 hardcover
ISBN 978-1-4473-6050-6 paperback
ISBN 978-1-4473-6051-3 ePub
ISBN 978-1-4473-6052-0 ePdf

Cover design: Clifford Hayes
Front cover image: Brian Barnes
Bristol University Press and Policy Press use environmentally
responsible print partners.
Printed in Great Britain by CMP, Poole

This book is dedicated to Suzy and our grandchildren, from oldest to youngest, Charlie, Abigail, Mattie, Adam, Ryan, Poppy, Evie, Martha, Elsie, Isobel and Amy. If there's any hope at all for planet Earth and all of us upon it, then it lies with future generations like theirs, who hopefully will have more say over the ideologies they live with than we have so far managed to achieve. All strength to them and I hope this book will help them!

Contents

About the author

Peter Beresford has long worked in the field of participation and citizen involvement as a writer, researcher, service user, activist and educator. He is Visiting Professor at the University of East Anglia, Emeritus Professor of Social Policy at Brunel University London and of Citizen Participation at the University of Essex. He is Co-Chair of Shaping Our Lives, the national user-led organisation which works for the rights and say of disabled people and service users. He is a long-term user of mental health services and also Visiting Professor at Edge Hill University.

Acknowledgements

Writing this book has felt like trying to take one more big step in making sense of increasing people's say and involvement in their lives and worlds. This has been my life's work and during the course of it I have incurred many debts, gained many colleagues and friends, and learned much from others. It simply is true that I – like the rest of us working to increase people's participation – would never have got to where I am without the help of very many others. As ever, there are many people I have to thank for whatever is good about this book. So I need to say a big general thank you. I also need to thank the team at Policy Press, particularly Ali Shaw for having faith in this book and bringing it to fruition, to everyone in Shaping Our Lives for all they have made possible, and to colleagues over many years at Brunel University London, the University of East Anglia and the University of Essex. Thank you all my friends and colleagues in the disabled people's and survivors' movements for all I have learned from you and working together, and not least my many Twitter friends who prove that social media can be a source of knowledge, strength, understanding, wisdom and support as well as cause for complaint. Thank you to all the students and colleagues I have worked with at universities who have shown real commitment to people's participation. Thank you yet again to my partner Suzy Croft for all her help and support, even as she worked as a welfare rights worker to support disabled people victimised by 'welfare reform'.

I also want to thank the reviewers of earlier versions of this book. Particularly I want to thank one of them, Lee Gregory. He went more than the extra mile. I was totally guided by him in undertaking the revisions I made to my first draft, not least after our daughter Ruth said she agreed with everything he said – and he also helped me with advice afterwards in preparing the revised draft, suggesting references and so on.

I additionally want to thank the community artist Brian Barnes for giving permission for his wonderful much loved Brixton mural, Nuclear Dawn, to feature in the book's cover design.

Finally, I must return to Ruth. This time if there is one person who stands above all others in the debt I have to her, that is Ruth Beresford, our daughter. Like me, Ruth has a profound interest in involvement. It was she who first suggested to me the importance of exploring the relations of ideology with participation, the focus of so much of my work. More and more I realised how right she was to highlight this issue. It became increasingly apparent that, as far as enquiry and action were concerned, political ideology was a dead zone for involvement. This was too big a debt to ignore. I asked Ruth if she would like to co-author the book as I felt its whole inception was owed to her. But this was in the middle of her PhD and Ruth clearly has her own row to hoe. She helped me develop the idea, wrote helpful notes which guided my thoughts, read a first draft and expressed her preparedness to do more. But in the end decided she did not want to be a co-author. This is a brave and generous act. I think she did more than enough to qualify, but I also think she wants to be her own person and I have to respect that. So all I can do is offer a big thank you and make clear her significant contribution. Thanks Ruth and everyone. I hope I can be as helpful to you one day!

Foreword

Yasmin Alibhai-Brown
Journalist, author and professor, Middlesex University

Ideologies vary and are, by definition, conflictual and defined by real or imagined enemies. They are divisive, demanding, enclosed and tribal. It is important to note, however, that even the most divergent are identical in the way they frame reality and fuel up on certainties. Anyone who has been to gatherings of single-minded activists knows this well. To query statements, make critical enquiries or express doubts is considered blasphemous. I have often emerged from these, not glowing with participatory validation, but feeling gagged and misrepresented. Over the years I have been damned as not left-wing enough, not black enough, not Muslim enough, not British enough.

And yet, without underpinning political and economic ideologies, democracies and societies would become fatally atomised and individualised. We see some of this today in the United Kingdom when voters complain that their particular preferences are 'being ignored' by 'elites'. I even had one reader of my columns write to me: 'I didn't fucking vote for people like you to come to my country. So why are you here?' The competition between capitalism and socialism, Labour and the Tories, faith and atheism, nationalism and internationalism keeps open societies dynamic and interactional. That we had the right, left and centre all committed to established rules of conduct in politics made for stability and continuity.

In a representative democracy, the majority elect the government, which is then expected to govern fairly and rationally, make evidence-based policies – even if unpopular – and look after the interests of the nation. For example, ever since the Empire Windrush docked at Tilbury Docks in June 1948, a sizable proportion of Britons have opposed 'coloured' migration. Yet every government since then has talked the anti-immigrant talk, but has not fully respected this will of the people because of economic imperatives. So, the angry chap above was right – people like him never wanted people like me in 'their' country. Their views did not, could not, prevail. The system is like a hanging mobile, maintaining a careful balance between government, parliament, the media and the people. That delicate balance has been destabilised since 2016. Disruption has been injected into the body politic.

Since the start of the Brexit battles, we have seen new ideologies fighting it out; populism and nationalism versus cosmopolitanism and social/economic liberalism. The latter is losing the battle. Nigel Farage whipped up an emotional storm in the hearts of Britons who felt they were ignored and marginalised. Citizen participation coming out of a sense of grievance, exploited by manipulative and unethical leaders, does not lead to benign outcomes.

The problem is not that the elites don't listen. It's that for most of the past quarter of a century, politicians have prioritised the upper and middle classes. In this class-ridden country, the poor and powerless have been rendered poorer and more powerless by the proponents of neoliberalism, from Thatcher, through Blair, Nick Clegg and David Cameron, to the right-wing cabal now in charge.

The fall of communism led to further hubris in the Anglosphere. Francis Fukuyama pronounced the end of history (1989). Western cutthroat capitalism was seen and sold as the only way to human progress.

The market was turned into an established religion; privileging the privileged, planned inequality its central tenet. Winners had it all, and there would be a trickle-down effect to benefit losers.

Extreme poverty was indeed reduced, but from the inhumanely low base of $1.90 per day per person. According to the World Bank, 'Fewer people are living in extreme poverty around the world, but the decline in poverty rates has slowed, raising concerns about achieving the goal of ending poverty by 2030 and pointing to the need for increased pro-poor investments.' The number of super-billionaires grows and welfare budgets are savagely cut, year on year. Neoliberalism has corrupted capitalism itself and has been spread around the world with impunity. Today the super-rich in Mumbai, Lagos, New York and London are comrades, socio-political brothers and sisters with a manic commitment to small states and minimal taxation for the richest, power and influence without responsibility.

Those at the receiving end are under tremendous pressure and understandably blame politicians, the 'undeserving', most of all foreigners. That leads to participation based on resentment and, sometimes, hate, and a drift into the orbs of UKIP and its satellites.

How can divisive, mournful and reactionary participation be turned into a truly effective counterforce to the ideologies of neoliberalism, neofascism and neonationalism?

This book begins to explore those big questions. It provides invaluable analysis and opens up possibilities in these darkly pessimistic times.

#MeToo, Black Lives Matter and Extinction Rebellion went global because they meant something to and roused millions of men, women and children around the world. All the movements originated in the West – just as neoliberal capitalism did – but they were moral causes which shook people out of debilitating passivity. That new energy cannot be disregarded by politicians, business, the media or other sectors. It shows that when diverse peoples come together for a common cause, find their voices and get engaged, they do change the world.

Peter Beresford is onto something big.

Preface

> The certainties of one age are the problems of the next.
> R.H. Tawney, English social historian and
> ethical socialist, 2016 [1922]

The COVID-19 pandemic, Black Lives Matter and #MeToo movements and renewed action against climate change all highlight grassroots pressure for political and social change on a global level. All are opposed by the international rise of market-driven neoliberalism and Right-wing populism. This growing conflict also spotlights the increasing gulf between narrowly based dominant political ideologies and popular demands for social justice, peace, environmentalism and human rights. Such grassroots campaigns have many different origins and expressions. But what they largely have in common is a desire to have more say and control over prevailing policies and values.

This book connects with this global intellectual and political challenge by examining for the first time the exclusionary nature of prevailing political ideologies. It does this at a time of rising interest in grassroots, citizen and service user participation in academic, research, policy, professional, political, social and cultural agendas. It not only offers a detailed critique of how we have got to present approaches to ideology and their limitations, but the crucial importance of moving to more participatory approaches, as is now recognised more generally for public policy and practice, and how this may be achieved.

The popular struggles now taking place and forcing themselves into news headlines and all our consciousness are not the one-minute wonders some of their critics might have hoped to dismiss them as. They have deep roots in history. The #MeToo movement's first high profile expression connected it with Hollywood and show business, where a long history of marginalising and abusing women was institutionalised in ugly clichés like 'the casting couch'. But the #MeToo movement had its origins in –and rapidly gained mass profile and support for highlighting – the pervasiveness of sexual abuse and assault in society (Fileborn and Loney-Howes, 2019).

Similarly, the Black Lives Matter movement did not come out of nowhere. Over many decades there has been a catalogue of attacks on African Americans by US police and a frequent matching failure of the criminal justice system to convict the guilty. We have been reminded that some of the important origins of US policing were patrols and night watches to catch runaway slaves, as well as the policing of segregation (Day, 2015; Horner, 2018; Brown, 2020).

These events have raised much bigger questions. What kind of society is it where the police seem routinely to attack and kill Black citizens rather than protect them? What kind of institutions are the US police and show business that physical and sexual violence and inequality seem to have become normalised and institutionalised within them? And in the UK, what kind of National Health Service has developed that, instead of saving lives, precipitately discharged many older and disabled people to domiciliary and residential care causing an estimated 30,000 plus deaths from COVID-19 (Savage, 2020)? What sort of values, what kind of organisational and political *ideologies* have been at the heart of this and why? Hopefully this book will begin to address and help us answer such questions.

A personal journey

I spent much of the first 2020 lockdown during the COVID-19 pandemic drafting this book. I have to say it was a great comfort to me to have this simple, if demanding, routine at a time of personal, national and global health emergency. And then on 25 May, George Floyd, an African American, was killed during arrest by a white policeman kneeling on his neck for almost eight minutes. These are events 2020 is likely to be remembered for. Both are likely to have massive and enduring consequences internationally. Both connect closely with the focus of this book.

After George Floyd's killing, protests against police violence towards Black people spread across the world under the banner of Black Lives Matter. COVID-19 prompted very different political and public health responses in different countries, some much more effective than others. Thus the responses in New Zealand, Taiwan and South Korea have been held up as examples of policymakers behaving speedily and efficiently to reduce the risk of infection, with their populations generally complementing this by acting sensibly and responsibly. It has been a different story in the UK, Brazil and the US, where the death rate has been disproportionately high and the policy response slow and ineffective (Saad-Filho, 2020; Cowper, 2020). Why such radical differences between different societies; what does this tell us about their institutions, their politics, their *ideologies*?

I have spent much of my working and thinking life concerned with the issue of *participation*. As I have often written when asked for a brief biography, I have a longstanding interest and involvement in issues of participation as a service user, researcher, educator, activist and writer. I have spent many years trying to make sense of participation – involvement, user involvement, citizen involvement – and the many other names it goes by. I have explored its policy, practice, theory, philosophy, knowledge base – and indeed attitudes underpinning it. It has been a long unfinished journey, one that can never be expected to be completed, learning from my own experience, the efforts of other people, working with them, mining the knowledge we have, critiquing and investigating it with others to reveal more.

I also began to realise, as the years went by, that it wasn't just me who was interested in people having more say in their life and world. More and more people similarly seemed to have a preoccupation with participation and making things more participatory. I saw this massive expansion of enthusiasm happening in relation to politics, policy, culture, services and research, and to the individual and their personal life. I saw it particularly coming from people and groups facing marginalisation. While it wasn't often the focus of prevailing political accounts of society, which seemed instead to reflect and focus on the shift to the political Right from the mid 1970s, there was certainly a significant if hidden history where participation was much more central (Beresford, 2019b).

Again, for me personally, perhaps most important was being able to think more about the intentions and objectives underlying participation. Why did people want it? Why did some others seem reluctant to let them have it? Did we all have the same vision for it? These are questions, I came to realise, about the *ideology* of participation; that is to say, the ideas and values that operate in societies. This was an issue which I increasingly found tended to be ignored in mainstream discussions about participation, but which seemed likely to be of central importance. Why we do something shapes how we do it, what it is, what it does and how helpful it is likely to be. The same, of course, is true of participation.

Then I had a small flash of insight! I was getting a clearer idea of the underlying motivations and purposes of participation, but this concept – ideology – I was really only scratching its surface. I needed to find out more about it. Participation, ideology – these are big ideas, like 'society' or 'the family'. We are unlikely to prosper if our examination of them is superficial – and so I tried to learn more.

Suddenly something else occurred to me, with some helpful outside prompting – my second moment of insight! If I needed to consider participation in relation to ideology, given the significance of ideology for participation, then surely dealing with such big ideas, similarly

I needed – we all needed – to consider *ideology in relation to participation*. It might have been a short step from realising I had to understand participation in relation to ideology to recognise that similarly I needed to understand more about ideology in relation to participation. But why hadn't I thought of this before?

I thought that lots of other people must have had the same idea. But as I tried to find out more, I realised that this wasn't the case. So I tried to think it through more for myself, writing an initial draft of this book. And the first time I did this, kind reviewers pointed out that I needed to know a lot more about ideology before I started pontificating about participation in relation to it. And this is what I have been trying to do, during lockdown and since, in what I am now offering. I hope I have been able to do this more helpfully now – in this exploration of two of what I believe are the most important ideas and influences on our lives. That is the theory and practice – the *praxis* – of participation and ideology, and the nature of their relationship.

It was probably Carole Pateman, the feminist academic, who first seriously raised the question of 'the place of "participation" in a modern theory of democracy' (Pateman, 1970, p 1). This was at a time, the late 1960s, when students and workers had not just become more interested in participation as an academic issue, they were also demanding it in their educational studies and workplaces – and far beyond – through large-scale international political movements and protests.

This book is not meant to be any kind of last word on the subject of participation and ideology. Rather the hope is to open discussion on the issue and encourage it to develop much further. I hope readers will see the book as such, recognise that it is offered with humility, and make their own contributions to take this debate forward. I believe it is especially important at this highly ideological time in world affairs, when major – often worrying and threatening – changes in political ideology emphasise the importance of all of us having some better understanding of ideology than we might as yet have gained.

Introduction

Not everything that is faced can be changed. But nothing can be changed until it is faced.

James Baldwin, 1924–87, writer,
poet and activist, quoted in Li, 2020

This book is concerned with ideology, different ideological perspectives, our relationship with them, and how we may change that for the better. It is particularly concerned with political ideologies. These are two words that for many people may be more likely to feel alien and difficult than comfortable and familiar. Yet political ideologies affect all our lives, in many cases very deeply. While we may not realise it, it is difficult for any of us to escape ideologies for even a minute. They may seem like a distant, abstract idea, but they can enter every aspect of our lives, impacting in life and death ways. The big thing about ideologies is that we may not realise we are being influenced by them or even that we have them.

The book's aims

A key aim in this book, therefore, is to make connections between two ideas which seem to have increasing significance for us all: participation and ideology. While they seem to be closely interrelated and to have major implications for each other, so far efforts to explore the relationship of the two seem to have been limited. The purpose of this book is to change that. Both these concepts are important for politics and public/social policy. However, while some attempt has been made over recent years to look at the ideological underpinnings of public participation (for example, Simmons et al, 2009), the same has not been true of participation in relation to ideology. Yet, as will emerge, this can be seen as a major gap in the discussion of ideology, especially given the massive literature that has developed about it – and the intersecting interest in participation. It is almost as if it has been seen as unproblematic for the ownership of ideology to be narrow and unconsidered.

This lack of attention to participatory approaches to ideology is all the more interesting and surprising given the rising political and policy interest in participation itself. The latter in turn seems to cross over traditional distinctions between left and right of centre politics.

Thus, on the one hand, has emerged what has come to be called the Right-wing populism associated, for example, with Donald Trump in the US, Boris Johnson and Nigel Farage in the UK, and Viktor Orban in Hungary, although it has become an almost global expression of modern national(ist) politics. On the other hand, we have witnessed rising grassroots pressure for participation from identity, service user, community and other new social movements, pressing for more direct say in society.

While much more attention has been paid to Right-wing populism than grassroots activism, both challenge conventional politics and highlight their limitations and disconnect from the grassroots. However different these two expressions of pressure for participation may seem, both present themselves in terms of groups experiencing exclusion and disempowerment; Right-wing populism in terms of white male blue-collar workers whose political, social and economic power has been eroded, and new social movements in terms of groups identifying as marginalised, facing discrimination and often denied the full rights of citizenship – women, LGBTQ, Black and minority ethnic communities, and disabled people. In both cases people are demanding a greater say in politics and policy and this pressure is creating a commensurate interest in issues of participation.

This book should be seen as a product of such interest. It is offered as a companion volume to *It's Our Lives*, which was concerned with supporting people's involvement and empowerment by valuing their knowledge and experience (Beresford, 2003). This book is similarly concerned with valuing people's knowledge and experience, but particularly in relation to the issue of ideology. Where the previous text was concerned with exploring participation in relation to research and knowledge production, here the focus is people's participation in the production and operation of ideology.

Ideology may be a word that many of us don't feel familiar or comfortable with, but the argument here is that it shapes all our lives. Just as earlier in *It's Our Lives*, we found that people's experiential knowledge seemed to be neglected and devalued in knowledge production, where much more value was attributed to so-called 'expert' knowledge, so it seems that people's lived experience and the knowledge arising from it largely play little if any part in the development of ideology, which nonetheless can massively and intimately affect all of us.

This seems highly problematic, as it means that prevailing ideologies are likely to be outside people's control, don't necessarily bear much relationship to their rights, interests and concerns, and ultimately can be used in ways that may be damaging and destructive to them.

Different ideological perspectives are often presented as though they reflect and are guided by our rights and needs, but how likely is that to be if we have little say in them? As we shall see, this can go for both ruling ideologies and those that seek to challenge them. Of course, it can't simply be said that just because you have no say in an ideology it is likely to be bad for you. But what does seem a much more helpful starting point is that an ideology people do have a say in is more likely to be in line with their rights and needs.

The aim here is to develop a different way of thinking about ideology and ideological perspectives and our relationship with them. This starts from the premise that if the aim is to advance an ideological perspective which promotes an empowering society and reflects everyone's rights and needs, then this is more likely to be achieved if it is done in a participatory way. This builds on my earlier hypothesis in relation to knowledge production. This stated that: 'The greater the distance between direct experience and its interpretation, then the more likely resulting knowledge is to be inaccurate, unreliable and distorted' (Beresford, 2003, p 4). This challenged the conventional assumption in positivist research that the opposite was true and that the *greater* the distance between direct experience and its interpretation, then the more reliable resulting knowledge is likely to be.

The proposition to be explored here is that:

> The more people are involved in the production of ideology about how a society should be, then the less it is likely that ideology and the society in which it is located will be oppressive, as opposed to, the more that ideology is imposed on them about how society should be, the more oppressive it is likely to be.

First, though, we have to re-examine the focus of discourse on ideology, which as yet does not seem to have been directed at such issues. In this text, the initial aim is to find out more about conventional discussions of ideology.

The structure of the book

To address its set task, the book is divided into three parts. These focus in turn on ideology, participation and challenging dominant ideologies through participatory action. However, what unifies the book – the thread running through it – is the relationship between ideology and participation. It is a thread that barely seems to have been considered until now. Unless we do so though, how can we fully understand ideology or participation or indeed advance progressive versions of either?

To this end, we begin in Chapter 1 by exploring the conventional discussion of ideology, focusing on political ideology to find out more about its origins and history, as well as the meanings attached to it and key forms it has taken. We familiarise ourselves with the 'expert' discourse on the subject and look at the idea itself, how it has been shaped, its association with science and 'expertise'. Finally, we address the history of ideology and encounter one that is essentially exclusionary rather than participatory.

In Chapter 2 we take the next step and focus on ideology's relations with 'us' – the people on the receiving end. Here the story seems to be one of a widespread lack of both familiarity and ease with the idea. Starting with the individual we explore how ideology impacts on us personally. We consider the idea of people's personal ideology, the forms it may take and what may shape it. We consider the ideological context of our individual experience, examining two extreme ideologies of the 20th century and the broader insights they offer as case studies.

Chapter 3 develops this discussion by asking if most of us play little part in shaping ideology what does. It does this by exploring the different forces and influences at work shaping our ideological preferences and how they are internalised. We look at the knowledge claims used to justify different ideological positions and how political ideologies serve as means as well as ends. Most important we focus on the ownership of ideology; where does it come from, what say do we have in it? We consider such questions also in relation to ideologies that have emerged to challenge ruling ideologies. Are they different, do we have more say in them? Are there exceptions to the rule?

In Part II of the book we come on to its main focus: reconnecting ideology and participation. We begin to look at a different approach to political ideologies, where the aim is to make possible our effective participation in them. Chapter 4 highlights that this represents a fundamental change in approach to ideology, one that begins with how we try to examine and discuss the concept. A central question is explored: is it possible for ideology to be liberatory unless it is participatory? We look at the insights for such participation to be found in the 'new social movements' that developed in the last quarter of the 20th century, including service user movements, and unpack participation considering its history, philosophy, models, contexts and meanings.

Chapter 5 focuses on the barriers that need to be addressed and overcome if such participation is to be inclusive and effective as a basis for a different approach to the development of ideology. The first of these issues to be addressed is power and inequalities of power, then we examine a range of routine exclusions and inequalities that can operate and how these can be challenged. The chapter explores a range of key requirements to ensure inclusive involvement, which include both support for the individual to be involved and improved access to previously excluding social institutions. In the first of two case studies, we see how disabled people got together to develop *their own* ideology, its key components and the emphasis they have placed on their participation.

In Part III we focus on making participatory ideology real. Chapter 6 moves on from individual involvement to how we can learn to work together to take collective action that maximises our power to bring about change. It continues to explore this from the perspective of disabled people and their movement because of the particular barriers and disempowerment they have successfully challenged and the broader insights this offers. We look at the pressures and circumstances that can operate to make people want to get involved and how we can take the first crucial steps to do this inclusively together, challenging individualisation and the limitations of traditional approaches to collective action.

Chapter 7 develops the discussion about working together by exploring how to have a real say – how we can develop our own organisations, as a basis for self-organisation, rather than merely serving other people's causes. We look beyond identity politics and the limitations associated with them, to focus on organising on the basis of shared experience, particularly of discrimination and exclusion. This provides a basis for self-organising around common understandings and strongly internalised goals arising from the desire to challenge oppression. We return to the self-organising of disabled people, which has highlighted the difference between traditional processes where non-disabled people controlled the agenda and one where disabled people seek to speak and act on their own behalf, setting up and controlling their own organisations. We see this also through the case study of such a 'user-led organisation', Shaping Our Lives, in which the author has been actively involved. Like other self-run organisations, it has done things differently to achieve different objectives, offering helpful insights for advancing participatory ideology in practice.

In order to take forward participatory ideology, we have already had to explore other key concepts, including power and difference. In Chapter 8 we focus on three further ideas and issues that are key for advancing participatory ideology. These are empowerment, language and knowledge, and in this chapter we examine each in more detail. First, though, we focus on theoretical discussion of making social and political change, as this is at the heart of this book's project.

Then we examine the concept of *empowerment*, a unique two-part idea for making change, which highlights the need for personal change as a prerequisite for participation in political change. We trace the idea's origins, its conceptualisation, different meanings, and what works to make it possible. We then look at *language* and its importance for ideology; how it is used to reinforce inequalities, impose power and manipulate people and how this has been and can be challenged. Finally we investigate *knowledge*; the role it has long been given to legitimate ruling ideologies, and how revolutionary and new social movements have highlighted and challenged this. We explore the emergence of experiential knowledge as an important part of this challenge and the important role it serves in helping to democratise knowledge and political ideology.

In the concluding Chapter 9, we pull together the arguments and the issues for democratising ideology. Having raised and explored the hypothesis that exclusionary ideology is unlikely to achieve emancipatory goals, we highlight the centrality of people working to achieve more say in society to work for more liberatory societies and a more sustainable planet.

Why ideology should be important to us

Of course, it may be suggested that we can all get along quite well without concerning ourselves with ideology. There are enough things to worry about, without adding to the list! On the other hand, being subject to something that can have massive consequences for your life, that you don't know much about and have little say in, does not seem a very safe place to be.

We also seem to be living at a time of increasing ideological conflict and extremism. That seems to be happening in terms of the day-to-day ideological threats facing people, as we have seen with large-scale resistance from the Black Lives Matter and #MeToo movements. But we are also seeing this globally, with more economic and military sabre rattling between the West, Russia and China. In the West, there was significant national and international ideological consensus after the Second World War with, for example, the creation of welfare states and the absence of major local conflicts. More recently we have moved far from that situation. Countries like the UK and the US seem to be politically polarised, with a populist Right still powerful but with some strong left of centre parties regaining traction too. There are many sites of war, enormous displacements of populations, and a prevailing neoliberalism that both impoverishes the Global South and exacerbates poverty and inequality in the Global North. Faith-based, tribal and post-colonial conflicts abound. Shifts in power from the colonial West to expansionist China, for example, are reflected in new struggles for rights and resistance like that of the Umbrella movement in Hong Kong. The ending of Soviet dominance in central and eastern Europe has been followed by renewed attacks on Roma, rising anti-Semitism and Islamophobia encouraged by aggressively racist Right-wing groups and administrations.

We can hardly ignore all these threatening signs, linked with large-scale death, destruction, disease and planetary damage. Ideology truly is all our business. Once we begin to think about ideological perspectives, a host of interesting questions come to mind. What does it all mean for us? Where do ideologies come from? Can they be helpful? Each of us is likely to have some personal ideology of our own. But to what extent it is truly ours, or instead something others have given or imposed on us, is another story. Are we the masters and mistresses of ideologies or merely their servants? Our heavily ideological times are undoubtedly damaging for many people. If ideologies are out of control, how might that change? Can we be part of changing it?

These are the kind of issues which this book is concerned with and on which we hope to throw at least some light. Underpinning it is the fear that many millions have already died on the altar of ideological perspectives, and many more might do so. If we are to prevent this continuing to happen, then we must at least try and get a better understanding of such an enormous idea as ideology. A key aim of this publication is to examine the relation between ourselves and ideologies, to help us understand them, particularly political ideologies, as a basis for rethinking and perhaps even changing our response to them. In doing so, it is hoped that it will help us be more aware of the impact ideologies may have on us and how we act and think.

Only then are we really likely to make sense of their influence on us and be in a position to challenge this – if we want to. Here the argument is that ideologies are much too important to be left to ideologues and those who hire and control them. If we don't give ideologies our attention, others will and already are – and quite probably at our expense.

PART I

Exploring ideology

1

Ideology: an exclusionary idea?

ideology
ˌʌɪdɪˈɒlədʒɪˌɪd–/ *noun*
noun: ideology; plural noun: ideologies
1. a system of ideas and ideals, especially one which forms
the basis of economic or political theory and policy.

Google/OxfordLanguages

Defining ideology

The aim of this book is to encourage fresh debate about ideology
in relation to participation. But it is important as a starting point to
examine existing discussions of ideology. We are unlikely to make
much progress if we don't learn from what's already been done and is
already known. But this is no simple task. Not only is the aim to get
beyond existing discussions, in this non-expert author's view, such
discussions are also often complex and opaque. Nonetheless, they
demand investigation, if we want to take either discussion or action
on ideology forward in any helpful way. So the aim of this first part
of the book is to introduce the reader to the subject through a short,
but hopefully not simplistic, discussion of ideology drawing on the
existing literature. If there's one thing I've learned in attempting this
task, it is that while ideology may impact on all of us, in one way or
another, it is something few of us seem to feel at home with.

So here, you might say, is the background *science*. Even attempting
this task is complex because this field has developed its own massive
literature, its own lexicon and field of study. Even the people arguing
about ideology are, as might be expected, themselves coming from
an ideological position. Thus, it is not only that the content of their
discussion relates to ideology, but that it is also shaped by their particular
ideological affiliations and commitments.

Commonsense understandings

So what is ideology? As with all words that aren't in commonplace use, the first task is to define our terms. What does it mean? What domain does it delineate? This is easier said than done, as becomes clearer when we investigate what might be called the 'expert discourse' in the next section. But there is a constellation of meanings that tend to be attached to 'ideology'.

When we look up the word in dictionaries, the definitions they offer highlight ideology's relationship with values, beliefs and ideas. Thus:

- a body of ideas that reflects the beliefs and interests of a nation, political system, and so on, and underlies political action
- the set of beliefs by which a group or society orders reality so as to render it intelligible
- speculation that is imaginary or visionary
- the study of the nature and origin of ideas.

  (www.dictionary.com/browse/ideology)

These values, beliefs and ideas can shape the way we think and act, both as individuals and together. These may be ideas that an individual, group or society has. Indeed, one of the interesting things about ideology can be the difference between our own personal ideologies and those of the society, community or country in which we live. Thus ideology is a set of ideas and values that underpins what we do – and what is done to us.

However, we have to remember that ideology on its own does not and cannot do anything. It is meaningless if no one adheres to it. Ideology has no effect if it gains no support or cannot be imposed. Without power underpinning it, a political ideology is no more than one person's or group's thoughts, aspirations or intentions. Beyond that it has no independent existence or influence. It must either have power behind it from its proponents or have power invested in it by others. Thus ideologies and ideological perspectives are inextricably linked with *power* (Chomsky, 2015). Different ideological perspectives are wielded by humans to explain, justify or legitimise a political or social order. Ideology can be used to justify oppression, but it does not oppress in itself. This is an important reminder that, beyond being an idea, ideology has no independent existence. It doesn't do anything itself. It may be used to oppress or liberate. Ideology began as and continues to be an idea and, from this, have followed different ideological perspectives (Heywood, 2017; Wetherly, 2017).

Political ideology is identified as a certain ethical set of ideals, principles, doctrines, myths, or symbols of a social movement, institution, class, or large group that explains how society should work, and offers some political and cultural blueprint for a certain social order. Political ideologies are concerned with the wide range of concerns of a society, ranging from the economy, health and education, to social security, social welfare and immigration (Honderich, 1995, p 392). Ideology can mean much more than political ideology, but equally political ideologies have a habit of entering into every aspect of life, thought, ideas and behaviour, as we shall see later (Shorten, 2015).

We should not ignore the fact that some intellectuals seeking to analyse the status quo have long had ideologies in their sights. Political ideologies can be used to serve many different purposes. Thus the philosopher and political theorist Hannah Arendt, in her exploration of 20th century totalitarianism, highlighted how such regimes were presented in almost supra-human terms, as if their proponents were merely following the diktats of nature or history, arguing: 'The last century has produced an abundance of ideologies that pretend to be keys to history but are actually nothing but desperate efforts to escape responsibility' (Arendt, 1951, page unknown). The feminist bell hooks, in contrast, highlighted the liberatory potential of feminism in the context of domination and oppression:

> Feminism is the struggle to end sexist oppression. Therefore, it is necessarily a struggle to eradicate the ideology of domination that permeates Western culture on various levels, as well as a commitment to reorganizing society so that the self-development of people can take precedence over imperialism, economic expansion, and material desires. (hooks, 1984)

Checking out the 'expert discourse'

Perhaps unsurprisingly, when we check out the dedicated literature on ideology, 'nobody has come up with a single adequate definition of ideology … the term has a whole range of useful meanings, not all of which are compatible with each other' (Eagleton, 2007, p 1). The word ideology has different histories and different conceptual strands, which in some cases are irreconcilable.

It was not always expected or meant to be like this. We are taught that the term ideology originated in (the French) revolution, when the rationalists of the Enlightenment were searching for a 'science of ideas' with which to make sense of and negotiate the highly charged and changing times they were living in (Kennedy, 1979). We will return to this idea of ideology as 'science' shortly. So it was that, more than two centuries ago, the French philosopher Destutt de Tracy introduced the term ideology in order to denote a new discipline that would study 'ideas': '*ideologie*' (van Dijk, 2006, p 729). In modern political science, the notion is used in a more neutral, descriptive sense, for example, to refer to political belief systems (Freeden, 1996). We can seek to come up with a value-free, uncontentious definition like 'a body of ideas' or 'the social representation of a group or class'. But this is likely to leave out many of the characteristics and qualities theoreticians have associated with ideology (Freeden et al, 2013; Leach, 2015).

However, the term ideology has also long been used in a pejorative way, to devalue and cast doubt on the views and beliefs of others. This has a very long history, which can be traced back to Karl Marx and Friedrich Engels for whom ideologies were 'a form of false consciousness'; thus, the working class may have misguided ideas about the conditions of its existence as a result of their indoctrination by those who control the means of production (van Dijk, 2006, p 728).

Here is ideology serving to mystify and deceive. Ideologies are often presented as a negative. The word 'ideological' is used crudely and dismissively, sometimes as a term of abuse, as though it makes an argument or an issue less valid, less true. When politicians criticise something as 'ideological', it is often as a cheap insult, with them pretending that they are themselves not guided by ideology. This tradition is alive and well and continues in day-to-day discussion and on the pages of the Right-wing press, where describing someone or something as 'ideological' has become a means of rubbishing them/it or challenging their veracity (Eagleton, 2007; Telegraph View, 2020).

We also have to remember that there are different kinds of ideologies. For example, there are expert and professional ideologies such as educational, legal, religious, and health care ideologies, among others. In this book, we are concerned primarily with *political ideology*; that is, ideology where different – sometimes opposed – groups, power, struggles, and interests are at issue and where the political process is essentially an ideological process (van Dijk, 2006, pp 731–2).

Most discussions of ideology and political ideology seek to explain what the terms mean and to explore key different ideologies that have developed through history. We can learn from these what goes to make up an ideology and what various important ideologies stand for.

There has even been talk of the 'end of ideology', as though competing political value systems and conflicts between them were a thing of the past and there was now only one ruling set of ideas or way of thought. This started in the 1950s with US sociologists and their assumption of the post-war dominance of Western capitalist liberalism or *liberal democracy* – that is to say, a form of government where representative democracy operates in a market economy. However, this assumption was powerfully challenged in the 1960s by the emergence of an international revolutionary student movement and neo-Marxists who determinedly challenged prevailing political ideologies (Kumar, 2006, p 170). However, the spectre of an 'end to history', through the ending of competing ideologies of 'Left' and 'Right', was raised again by the US historian and political scientist Francis Fukuyama in the late 1980s (Fukuyama, 1992), following the fall of Soviet communism, with a significant disregard for the radical developments which were taking place in China, the Middle East and the Indian sub-continent. While this claim that we lived in a post-ideological age was used to give rhetorical force to developing US neoliberalism, it in turn came under heavy challenge, both intellectually and through international events. Later Fukuyama revised his timetable, but what he was really talking about was only the apparent ending of one form of ideology, Soviet communism (Menand, 2018). Political ideologies, if anything, continue to be alive and well, imposed with growing power and force.

There have also been suggestions that ideology has become less important and pervasive as technology and bureaucracy have developed and become more central (Habermas, 1971). However, neither of the latter can be seen as ideologically neutral and both can and have been used to serve ideological purposes. Thus, for example, the extension of bureaucratic control has been associated with marketisation and the advance of Western neoliberalism (Ritzer, 2008).

Writing in 2007, Eagleton commented on 'the remarkable fact that the concept of ideology should be out of fashion among intellectuals at just the time when it was flourishing in reality' (Eagleton, 2007, p xiii). I believe his words still hold true, perhaps more each day and as each new national and international political event takes place: 'Ideology has never been so much in evidence as a fact and so little understood as a concept as it is today' (Eagleton, 2007, dust jacket). Also it is difficult to think of many areas of human activity where history seems to have such a powerful, enduring and sometimes worrying and destructive effect as it seems to in relation to ideology. I should add that I say this both as someone who first studied and valued history as a university student and one of whose passions remains old motorcycles; their social, cultural and engineering past, restoration and renewal, their maintenance and use. So I'm not one to dismiss the importance of history. Reflecting particularly on my own 1940 BSA army despatch rider's bike, this encourages an interest in what has gone before. But the history of ideology – as both a field of study and area of human activity – not only excites this interest, but also seems to force itself into your consciousness as soon as you seek to address the subject in any way, imposing constraints and restrictions. It can feel a subject that is unable to escape its past. This is a history that is made difficult to ignore, which seems sometimes to preoccupy and entrap ideology's commentators and practitioners, where we constantly seem to be being punished for our forefathers' 'sins'.

The conventional history of political ideology is reminiscent of that we were taught of Western nations at school, except, instead of kings and queens, we are taken through lists of key political thinkers. Instead of royal houses and families, we learn about schools of thought.

Exploring the literature of ideology, particularly political ideology, has been a new and demanding task for me. It is both a complex and voluminous literature that it has felt hard work to get my head round. No wonder as we will see, it is often suggested that ideology is not an idea that seems particularly familiar or comfortable to many people. So the aim here is not to offer an exhaustive examination of the definition, nature and range of ideologies but rather to provide a starting point for setting off in a fresh direction. This text is not intended as a primer on political ideology, but rather an attempt to set us thinking about it in different ways. Of course, that means we have to get some handle on the conventional basics. Here we are trying to tread the difficult path of not getting lost in other people's definitions and agendas, when the primary aim is to explore how people more generally do and can connect with ideas of ideology. At the same time, we cannot ignore the need to explore the meaning of the idea if there is to be any kind of meaningful discussion about it.

Starting points: the history

Students of ideology adopt different starting points in their historical analysis of political ideology. The English revolution (or, as it is more often known, the English Civil War) of the 17th century is perhaps a particularly helpful one here for consideration of ideology in a

UK context. Not only is it a key ideological development in British history, when the economically emerging middle class challenged their restricted political power under absolute monarchy. It was also an early UK candidate for re-evaluation through the prism of Marxist ideology (Hill, 1940). However, we could also trace political ideology much further back, through feudalism and pre-feudalism, through mercantilism and then to the 'Enlightenment', industrialisation and post-industrialisation. More typically, we are taken through the history of great thinkers and political ideologists. This begins with liberals like Locke and Voltaire, believers in the social contract between state and citizens like Hobbes and Rousseau, conservatives like Edmund Burke and Chateaubriand, utilitarians like Bentham, Ricardo, Adam Smith and John Stuart Mill, the antecedents of Marx and Marxism, Kant and Hegel, post-Marxists like Touraine, Baudrillard and Bourdieu, and postmodernists like Lyotard and Foucault (Eagleton, 2007; Feuer, 2017).

Western Enlightenment interest in ideology was associated with liberal philosophy based on support for individual liberty, private property, the market and limited state power. Its most conspicuous expression, 'utilitarianism', offers an early warning against taking ideologies at face value. Utilitarianism's maxim was that 'the greatest happiness of the greatest number ... is the measure of right and wrong' (Burns and Hart, 1977, p 393). Given that it was the inspiration for the cruelty and harshness of the dreaded English New Poor Law introduced in 1834, imposed on many thousands of impoverished people, it actually seems to the present author, 'much more to have served the interests and be concerned with the greatest happiness of the small minority who governed and influenced the state, had the vote and ran the Poor Law' (Beresford, 2016, p 34). The 19th century also witnessed the emergence of Marxist, socialist and anarchist ideologies which not only offered radical alternatives to prevailing liberal ideology, but also powerful critiques of existing understandings of ideology. The original insight of Marxist thinking was that those who controlled the means of production shaped the ideology that was used to justify society. Since then, different theories have developed, like 'false consciousness', 'cultural hegemony' and lack of 'cultural capital', which highlight how such ideology can work to deflect the majority from their own best interests (Hawkes, 2003; Haralambos and Holborn, 2008; Heywood, 2013).

When philosophers like Hobbes and Rousseau posited their ideas on the 'state of nature', imagining how things were before human civilisation, they did so on the basis of their existing state of knowledge, not on what we might know now from archaeology, carbon-dating and the rest. Similarly their thinking was tied to contemporary racist, sexist, heterosexist and colonialist assumptions and ways of thinking. Such formulations, as Eagleton observed, thus involve 'epistemological questions', that is to say, 'questions concerned with our knowledge of the world'. As he goes on to say, some are 'preoccupied with ideas of true or false cognition, with ideology as an illusion, distortion and mystification' (Eagleton, 2007, pp 2–3). The focus of ideology's founding *fathers* (for it was so) was largely limited to Western Greco-Roman societies.

If we now pick up a modern text which is trying to help us make sense of political ideology, like the *Oxford Handbook* (Freeden et al, 2013), we can quickly see both the limits of past discussions and explorations of such ideology and how all embracing such study can and should be.

Thus as well as encountering the classic families of ideology, like conservatism, liberalism, social democracy, communism, Marxism, fascism, nationalism, republicanism, colonialism, anarchism, utopianism, we are also being acquainted with green, feminist, globalising, Islamic, Chinese, Modern African and South Asian and Southeast Asian ideologies (Freeden et al, 2013).

Ideology: the idea

Political ideology is a term fraught with problems, having been called 'the most elusive concept in the whole of social science' (McLennan, 1986, p 1). As has been said, it is difficult, not to say impossible, to develop serious discussion about any idea without clearly defining it. Yet it is difficult to do this with ideology since definitions are both multifaceted and heavily contested. They are also frequently described as value-laden and normative, which is hardly surprising, given that they often represent one or other kind of rationalisation, justification or analysis for action. Eagleton runs through most of the letters of the alphabet when he attempts to list some definitions of ideology (2007, pp 1–2). Thompson concludes that the single most widely accepted definition is to do with legitimating the power of a dominant social group or class, so in that sense its role is to 'sustain relations of domination' (Thompson, 1984, p 4) This is certainly how I have understood it to operate, in the way Eagleton defines: 'the process of legitimation … by promoting beliefs and values congenial to it; naturalizing and universalizing such beliefs so as to render them self-evident and apparently inevitable; denigrating ideas which might challenge it; excluding rival forms of thought ... and obscuring social reality in ways convenient to itself' (Eagleton, 2007, pp 3–4). Such definitions are also generalised to extend to any 'set of ideas by which (people) posit, explain and justify ends and means of organized social action, and specifically political action, irrespective of whether such action aims to preserve, amend, uproot or rebuild a given social order' (Seliger, 1976, p 11).

Furthermore, ideologists are not simply neutral commentators on ideology; they are also developers and creators of it. Thus thinkers like Gramsci help explain why people may support regimes antagonistic to their own interests (Gramsci, 1971) or Foucault the relations between state, society and understandings of madness and 'mental illness' – although the latter tends to talk more of 'discourse' than ideology (Foucault, 1988). At the same time, there long seems to have been a search for an objective or 'scientific' understanding of ideology, as though the idea and its exponents are separable from norms and values and are merely demarcating an area rather than passing judgement on something – for or against. The contents of ideology and the views of their analysts may be a matter of opinion, but they tend not to be presented as such. On the other hand, there are more and less objective definitions of ideology, the former usually narrowly framed in terms of the political and cultural blueprint for a certain group or order.

When we make an initial check on the literature, for example, through Google Scholar and Researchgate, it seems to confirm that discussion exploring ideology and participation has been very limited. While, as we might expect, there is some focusing on the ideology of participation/involvement, there is much less examining participation in relation to ideology, particularly in relation to political ideology. One apparent exception is work by Douglas Ashford, although his focus is more specifically on the relationship of ideas to political behaviour (Ashford, 1972). He has also come in for criticism as more narrowly concerned with exploring major psychological approaches to the study of political behaviour (Cobb, 1973). Interestingly though, he seems to see people's relationship with ideology primarily as 'followers', rather than initiators or co-creators, reinforcing conventional understandings of ideology as narrowly based.

Ideology's non-participatory past

This book by contrast is primarily concerned with making the connections between participation and ideology. This seems to be a particularly timely project because of the widespread and growing interest in public and service user participation in all aspects of life, including politics and policy, and because of the complex inter-relations that connect these two key ideas – ideology and participation. Yet, when we come to investigate ideology, we encounter a very different history, with little apparent interest in participation. It is this we begin to examine next, as we embark on what seems like an unprecedented journey of discovery.

What is most striking is that ideology and its development rarely seems to have been understood as any kind of participatory process or project. This appears to be the case right from the start. As the Right of centre writer Ferdinand Mount reminds us, the creation of the idea of ideology was associated with a companion word 'ideologues', the intellectuals and theoreticians who advanced the discourse. Thus, in one sense, ideology has been private property from the start or at least a very narrowly based activity (Mount, 2012, p 112–3). As Mount said, Destutt de Tracy (who, as we have seen, coined the word ideology) conceived it as another science, one in which the young needed to be instructed. Thus the process of its development was a top-down one – with ideology a prescription 'deduced from the principles of the Enlightenment [based on] the correct political ideas' (Mount, 2012, p 113). Ideology was something people would be taught, rather than being actors in its formation.

But there's another sense in which de Tracy seems to be laying the ground for preconceiving ideology as essentially an idea beyond being participatory. This is his emphasis on it as 'scientific'. Again to quote Mount:

> [de Tracy's] primary epistemological claims – that ideology is a science, that from the principles of this science a uniquely valid social and political programme can be deduced, and that both the principles and the programme can and must be taught to the nation's young and enforced by the state – these claims we shall meet again. (Mount, 2012, p 113)

Such claims occupy a particularly significant place in 20th century thought. Philosophers like Kant and Hegel reinforced notions of ideology as scientific. Following in their footsteps, Karl Marx also believed ideology to be a science, with its own scientists. Both Nazi and Soviet communist ideology were similarly conceived in such objective scientific terms. The rest of us are cast as the recipients rather than potential co-creators of political ideology, ultimately subject to its enforcement, rather than entitled to reinterpret or challenge it. It is invested with the authority attached to positivist scientific enquiry, as if it is based on the same kind of objective truths as natural science. Only its scientists are entitled to explore and experiment with it.

Keith Harrison and Tony Boyd extend this idea of the relationship most of us have with ideology as an essentially passive one, when they write about the *transmission* of ideology and people as merely empty vessels, or the 'receptors' for it, rather than actors with agency involved in any sense actively with it in a two-way process (Harrison and Boyd, 2003, p 143–5). As they discuss, this of course connects with those understandings of ideology simply as an instrument of power wielded by the dominant groups in society, even to the extent of 'enslaving' those who accept or believe in it. This is the very opposite of any kind of understanding of ideology as a collaboration between those who inspire it and those who support it, let alone any kind of co-production. An even more developed view of this, as these authors suggest, is where people's influence on ideology is seen to be reduced by spin doctors and modern methods of communication (Harrison and Boyd, 2003, p 145).

An ultimate expression of this is *propaganda*, where people are essentially induced to believe in whatever misrepresentations, exaggerations or indeed lies, power holders choose to feed them.

Humphrey and Umbach (undated) develop the discussion about the relationship between political ideology and propaganda. Umbach, from her historical work, highlights how this can be a two-way process, but one where the individual is essentially subordinate to the dominant ideology, even though they may engage with it. As she also reports, while propaganda must engage with lived experience to carry conviction, it tends to manipulate and distort this (Humphrey and Umbach, undated). The ultimate objective of propaganda is to make people think and act as its proponents want, even if this means deceiving them, rather than supporting them to think for themselves.

However, going back to the early idea of ideology as science, we can also see an apparent contradiction almost built into it. As Ferdinand Mount reminds us, de Tracy, while committed to this notion, also regards our subjective or 'sense experience (as) the only reliable knowledge that we can have of the world ... The idea that our senses could delude us ... is quite foreign to [him] ... So the ambiguities of ideology were inbuilt from the start' (Mount, 2012, p 114). We will return to this epistemological issue relating to ideology later, when we explore the possibilities of its participatory development.

The political and academic worlds of ideology, as this author has been discovering, are complex and dense. They can be difficult to understand. This also seems very much a private province, explored by few. That might not be by intention, but it is certainly likely to be true for many newcomers. No wonder the frequent suggestion that it is unfamiliar territory for many of us. This is our starting line for enquiry in Chapter 2, when the focus on the relations between political ideology and the people it can affect really starts.

2

Ideology and us

Ideologies separate us. Dreams and anguish bring us together.

Eugene Ionesco, playwright,
quoted in Safransky, 1990

Having started the journey of exploring political ideology in relation to participation, our next step is to examine it in relation to the people it affects – that is to say *all of us*. So far, the emphasis in expert discussion seems to have been on the *nature* of ideology – what it is and what it is for – rather than on its social construction and ownership. The restricted scope of the latter either seems to have been seen as in the nature of ideology or taken for granted. It is almost as if it has been regarded as unproblematic for the ownership of ideology as an idea and activity to be narrow. There has been little exploration of the whys and wherefores of this. But this lack of interest in our relationship with political ideology and how much say we do or don't have in it does seem interesting. Is this a wise course of action? Is it really such a good idea to be so disconnected from a concept with such potential power over us?

The fact that discussion about ideology and specific ideologies or ideological approaches has been narrowly based does not seem to have attracted much mainstream comment or attention. How readily would we accept this of any other issue with such dramatic and far-reaching implications? Also, at a time when there is so much high profile resistance to attacks on particular groups' rights and so much interest in broader participation, we have to ask how much longer can we ignore the issue of people's involvement in the development of political ideology – especially when it has so much impact on all of us and people seem increasingly to want to have more say over the policies and politics that affect them? Given its potential importance in our lives we might expect that political ideology would routinely be seen as a priority concern for people. But that does not seem to have been the case.

The implications for us

As soon as we start thinking about ideology, a worrying contradiction quickly becomes apparent. That something potentially as important as ideological perspectives may be something we know little about seems both highly significant and also troubling. This raises big questions. If we haven't had the chance to reflect on or engage with ideologies, yet they can have such an impact on us – personally, socially, economically, politically and even psychologically, what conscious say, what control do we actually have over them? Do they operate on us like a hidden hand? Do we know what we are signed up to? Are we made passive repositories for ideologies rather than active agents in their construction? Does this challenge our beliefs about free will and democracy? This really sounds like something that we need to give serious reconsideration to.

We can make few assumptions about ideology as an idea or ideologies as political drivers. It is not even as though some of us at least don't show some interest in or understanding of the idea. So, for example, when I asked people on Twitter what ideology meant to them, their comments reflected face value and conventional definitions, but also said more, for example:

- A set of core beliefs about how things should be done, often used as a short-cut to avoid issue-by-issue consideration.
- All our political parties pretend they are ideology-free. Values have given way to watered down notions of 'what works'.
- Representing a feminist organization, I get labelled as 'ideological' as though other organisations in the room are not: but they are of course, it's just that their ideology is accepted without thinking.
- A theory of how society should be. Idealism: valuing your ideology above people. Beware the idealistic ideologue.
- I'm driven by an ideology fashioned by my existence, faith and hopefulness and driven by passion for Vocation.
      (Twitter responses to author, various accounts)

Once we start looking at and thinking about political ideologies, we begin to appreciate that there can be patterns within them. Certain attitudes seem to go together, for example, belief in capital punishment, people looking after themselves rather than expecting 'the state' to look after them, opposing abortion and having a hard-line attitude to crime, tend to form little clusters or constellations that regularly recur (see for example, Filipovic, 2019). Similarly, commitments to state support, more liberal penal policy and restrictions on military intervention often go hand in hand. In this they reflect broader historical political positions associated with the 'Right' and the 'Left'. But these aren't unchanging. For example, under the hard Right UK Conservatism of Margaret Thatcher, legislation was introduced to oppose learning and support for LGBTQ issues. Now the Tory Party has formally rejected such discrimination, and politicians who would once have been 'closet gays' are now 'out' and in positions of power and importance.

But there are unexpected conflicts relating to ideology. At school our children are taught to be kind to each other and to animals, to respect the environment and not to be selfish or greedy. Yet we live in a world where brutal conflict and competition extending to the violence of war and civil conflict and the ravages of poverty, want and environmental destruction seem to be accelerating. What explains such massive contradiction? Why is it so often we seem more prepared to spend money on killing rather than looking after each other?

Thus we learn that ideologies can take many forms; they involve both conscious and unconscious ideas, are highly politicised, closely connected with power and extend into both the public and personal spheres. Debate about ideologies and ideological perspectives is complex and contentious. They seem to enter into everything.

Ideologies can be concerned with how things are done as well as what they are done for. But as well as being associated with different models of society and social goals (Freeden, 2006), they can also be associated with different understandings of human beings and 'human nature'. Thomas Hobbes's philosophy in the 17th century was based on a pessimistic understanding of human life as 'nasty, brutish and short' (Hobbes, 2016); Mahatma Gandhi's optimistic view was of the inherent goodness of people (Ragavan, 2000). The post-war UK welfare state was essentially based on a model of human beings as altruistic, while Tony Blair's 'New Labour' rested on an idea of human beings as essentially selfish (Russell, 2005; Beresford, 2016).

Ideology: starting with the personal

Whatever we think of it, however much or little we know about or are aware of ideology and ideological issues, we don't seem to be able to escape them. They seem to affect us all. It is this we turn to next, starting with our 'personal' ideology. This cannot be assumed to be an unproblematic concept in itself and will therefore demands careful examination. Nonetheless, as the closest that many of us might get to ideological analysis in our own lives, it seems a promising and helpful starting point. Given the aim here is to explore the relationship that we may have with ideology, particularly political ideology, it makes sense to start any enquiry with us – *ourselves*.

Personal ideology

Here we start with the view that people may not be familiar with the word ideology or even know whether they have an ideological perspective, but the likelihood is that they do, in terms of having their own structure of values and ideas. The idea of having a personal ideology is likely to make more sense to them if it is presented in terms of their values. Once we consider it more carefully, we can be surprised at how much our ideology can be both the same as and different to that of other people and with what it may be linked.

Thinking about our own personal ideology may also serve as a helpful way into a better understanding of the issue of ideology itself, and indeed into making connections with participation – this book's particular focus. We are not suggesting here that anyone's personal ideology is also a political ideology, but we will go on to explore how the two might be linked. Put simply, a personal ideology can be defined as how someone believes life should be led and what forces they see as influencing people's lives (de St Aubin, 1996, p 162). Beginning like this, with the personal, may be helpful in exploring ideology's relations with participation. First perhaps, it's worth asking ourselves the question: what is my ideology, my ideological perspective, and where do I think it comes from? Or putting it more simply and in more day-to-day language: what do I believe in; what are my values, what moral code do I feel guides or should guide me? This may be something someone has given a lot of thought to. Or maybe it is a question they have never asked themselves. We suggest readers try doing so now anyway and maybe make a note of what they think. It may be a good idea to come back to this later, when there's been time to read more of and reflect on this book.

My guess is that many people have never explicitly asked themselves these initial questions. They may not necessarily even have realised that there are questions to ask. They may not have actively chosen or adopted an ideology. It would be interesting to find out more about this, but research tends to be focused on what those who pay for it are interested in, rather than necessarily what it would be really helpful or important to know more about. Writing this book, it seemed an important question. Of course, some of us may have asked it, but in a different way, for example, wondering: what do I really believe in, where do I get my ideas from, how do I think I should bring my children up, how do I think things should be in the world and how might we achieve that?

Of course, having a personal ideology does not mean that it has any great power or force behind it – beyond perhaps being able to exert influence over your partner, children or your pets! In abusive relationships that, of course, may be power enough. But generally speaking, it is no more than a code of conduct for yourself. People may not even have the personal power to act in accordance with it, let alone impact on anyone else. Like any ideology, it only has life and force insofar as it has power behind it to enforce and maintain it (Therborn, 1999). Personal ideology should be recognised as being no more than that, unless it is associated with the power – personal, social, cultural or political – to impose it more broadly.

But this big and possibly unfamiliar word 'ideology' may put many people off asking the question we started with. If asked out of the blue, maybe we'd get answers like, 'What do you mean?', 'I don't really understand', or 'I've no idea'. We might also get a lot of people saying, 'I don't have an ideology'. And when you are asked about something you may not feel you know about or really understand and you worry about showing your ignorance or making a fool of yourself, that could be a truthful and very sensible answer.

However, all of us are likely to have some kind of ideological perspective or value system, it's just that we may not think of it like that. Similarly, we may discover that we have had an ideology *all* our lives. It's the beliefs and values we live our life by – day to day. What we believe, what makes up our ideology may vary enormously, but until proved otherwise, as far as we can see, all of us have some kind of value and belief system. It may have its origins in the Judaeo-Christian Ten Commandments, the Five Pillars of Islam, the Communist Manifesto, or a simple adage like 'Do as you would be done by'. We may never have articulated it. We may not often refer to it. It may be full of internal contradictions. But some kind of ideological system of beliefs and values is likely to lurk within us, guiding our thoughts and actions, affecting our 'conscience' or 'superego' – whether we abide by it or not. As author of this book, I take the view, until evidenced to the contrary, that everyone has some kind of ideology/ideological position, whether they know it or not, whether it is really, deliberately, theirs or not.

But even though our personal ideology may be highly individual and idiosyncratic, perhaps unique to us, it is not something that either operates in isolation or comes out of nowhere.

What shapes individual ideology

So where does this personal ideology come from? Some have tried to suggest that it is effectively in our genes. This was behind the invention of the 'F Scale', a 1947 personality test to measure 'the authoritarian' personality to see if you were a fascist (Adorno et al, 1950). During the Spanish Civil War, medical experiments were carried out by fascist nationalists in Francoist concentration camps on Left-wing republican prisoners to 'establish the bio-psych roots of Marxism' (Beevor, 2006, p 407).

We can expect to find more convincing explanations for our personal ideologies, however, in:

- our socialisation – for example, through our family upbringing, parental messages and the like;
- our formal education; our schooling and peer group;
- the time and place in which we live; the prevailing politics, culture and nature of our society;
- our location in it: our class, culture, ethnicity, gender, age, sexuality, disability, our friends, peer pressure, and so on;
- the strength, influence and nature of prevailing media and other sources of influence.

And so on … Others may have a different or indeed longer list. And, just as some external pressures might encourage us to internalise a particular set of values and beliefs, such pressures might equally lead us to rebel against beliefs. We have known children who grew up to be vegetarians because they disliked the meat eating of their parents, but equally children with vegetarian parents who chose to eat meat when they left the family home. Expert analyses also seem to be conditioned by their disciplines. Thus psychologists tell us that our ideologies reflect 'unconscious motivational processes' (Jost et al, 2008). Sociologists, meanwhile, relate ideologies to cultural beliefs that justify particular social arrangements, including patterns of inequality (Macionis, 2010).

Of course, we aren't just blank pieces of paper for others to stamp their values and ideas upon, so that we internalise and adopt them. On the other hand, we don't necessarily simply choose our ideological position. Instead, we can be expected to negotiate the influences that impact on us and end up with our own particular value mix. We won't all be the same. There is individual agency – our various capacities to mediate outside forces. But equally we know that powerful messages from politicians, policymakers, opinion formers (including institutions like the church and political parties) and the mass media, can have massive effects on us, influencing how we see the world, how we explain things and what we end up believing. The ancient Greek philosopher Aristotle's boast, 'Give me a child until he is seven and I will give you the man' (more often attributed to the founder of the Jesuits, Ignatius Loyola), sums this up. We also learn about the power of 'parental messages': things we learned at our parents' knees that we unthinkingly have taken as gospel.

Also we know that advertising and mass media work in complex and subtle ways. Newspapers like the *Daily Mail* and *Sun* have track records of support for Right-wing, even fascist, governments and dictatorships, but they demonstrate enormous skill in persuading their readers that they are on *their* side, understand their concerns, support their interests. They attack people on welfare benefits as scroungers and refugees as freeloaders, while their proprietors pay minimal tax by claiming non-domiciled status and retaining foreign citizenship (Philo et al, 2013). Yet they continue to be remarkably effective in dividing us; not against them, but against each other. There is no doubt that in the UK increasing hostility has been engendered against particular groups, notably people on welfare benefits and immigrants and asylum seekers, resulting in increased public hostility to them, with them increasingly being identified as problems and subject to rising hate crime (Philo et al, 2013). This has been as a result of the strength of Right-wing ideology in countries like the UK.

Some issues seem to be particularly susceptible to being 'ideologised' – if there is such a word. Of course, this varies with times and cultures, but some of the most enduring in societies like the UK have been:

- the death penalty
- abortion
- teenage pregnancy
- 'assisted dying'
- pornography

Interestingly many seem to be life and death matters, although that isn't necessarily the defining issue of such recurring focuses for headlines and divisiveness. These are issues we are encouraged to have strong opinions about. They are also issues where those strong opinions continue to be fostered even when significant policy changes have been made. In all cases, entrenched positions – encouraged by those with their own powerful ideological interests – make it that more heat than light tends to be generated about these issues.

So to sum up, we all of us are likely to have some kind of ideological position of our own, even if we aren't clear about this. We may play a part in shaping it, but our values are also likely to be heavily influenced by a wider range of social, cultural, political, economic, historical, media and personal pressures that operate on us. Personal and political ideologies exist in relation to each other, but these relationships can be complex, unexpected and power-related. Also, it cannot be assumed that everyone has had the opportunity to think and work through their own personal ideology, so that this reflects their particular desires and preferences, instead of being unconsciously or externally imposed on them.

So while we may play a more or less active part in shaping our personal ideology, all the signs are that it is likely to be heavily influenced by sources outside us. We may oversee the detailed mix of our internalised values and beliefs. However, we may have little hand in the overall process shaping prevailing ideologies and creating the context for our personal philosophy, even if we may make our own choices – more or less – over which we opt for. Also, the knowledge we have that helps shape our ideology may essentially be more or less mediated for us by socialisation, mass media and other influences, rather than independently arrived at on our own account.

Some of us, like the present author, may feel that they have been privileged, for example, by education and personal life chances, to have some opportunity to reflect on their individual ideology and actively articulate and shape it for themselves. However, the reality is that for many of us this may not be true. We may not be fully aware of 'our' ideological position or fully committed to it. If we haven't had much chance to consider or explore our own ideology, then it is quite likely to be inconsistent and contradictory. We may unconsciously be committed to contradictory beliefs. What we say may not be the same as what we do. There may be big internal inconsistencies between what we think we believe in. So, for example, we may think we are committed to treating people with equality, yet have internalised unthought-through prejudices against particular groups.

What else would explain the ease with which modern media and governments have been able to whip up popular hatred against groups like refugees, whose situation is clearly linked with structural issues like globalisation, civil war and genocide? We are not saying such inconsistencies are necessarily 'wrong' or unsustainable. But they do raise fundamental questions about the inherent viability of ideology that is unconsidered and unreflexive. There is another issue to raise about our personal ideology. However important and influential it might be to us, it is very unlikely – unless we are particularly important or influential or merely reflect some dominant ideology – to carry any significant power. We may think and be guided by it, but it is unlikely to carry any weight or exert any influence in the wider world we inhabit. It may be important in how we treat our cat or our children, but its power is unlikely to extend far beyond that.

This consideration of our personal ideology also raises another question. What understanding of and say are we likely to have in ideologies more broadly – those which are likely to shape and structure our lives – if we are not even clear about our own? That is one of the key issues we hope to explore in this book. Next we turn to some of the great historic political ideologies that have shaped our current context and understandings to help make better sense of this.

Our ideological inheritance

If ideology developed as a term and idea in the 19th century, political ideologies dominated people's lives in the 20th and brought many millions to an end through war, want and genocide. The 20th century can thus be seen as the age of ideology, and there is little sign that this has changed since. Different ideologies could now be spread deeper, faster and further in ways that hadn't existed before, through the emergence of popular press, photography, radio, film, television – and now, the internet and world wide web. Three ideologies, both overlapping and conflicting with each other, provided the backdrop in the 19th century to people's lives and understanding globally: nationalism, colonialism and (social) liberalism. Summed up briefly these can be defined as:

> **Nationalism**, an ideological position based on the premise that the individual's loyalty and devotion to the nation-state surpass other individual or group interests. Nationalism is a modern movement.
>
> **Colonialism** The ideology of colonization, based on the doctrine of cultural hierarchy and supremacy. ... Features of the colonial situation include political and legal domination over the 'other' society, relations of economic and political dependence, and institutionalized racial and cultural inequalities.

31

> **Social liberalism** is a political ideology that believes individual liberty requires a level of social justice. ... Social liberal ideas and parties tend to be considered centrist or centre-left. (Freeden, 2013)

Common insights from the ideological extremes

Two other key ideologies, however, also emerged in the 20th century. While we could also identify others (for example, Maoist communism and Wahhabist Islamism), these two and their relationship with each other have particular historical significance and ramifications for this discussion. Ostensibly totally antagonistic, their rise dominated the first half of the century and their fall shaped the second. They still seem to exert a powerful influence. Their imposition and antagonism resulted in the greatest war and the biggest slaughter in human history. These ideologies are fascism and Soviet Russian communism. They ended empires and created new ones. Neither could be said entirely to escape the bounds of the first three ideologies we identified. However, both could be seen to represent a fundamental challenge to them. While the funeral rites have now been said over both these political ideologies, they still exert an influence on the modern world, as a warning, threat and exemplar, and still find new nasty expressions – even if not on their former scale.

They also serve as high profile case studies, especially as the global war which brought them into direct conflict, in the UK at least, still seems to exert an undue fascination and influence on our understanding, through popular culture, the national curriculum and remembrance. What particularly interests this author is that these two ideological perspectives were essentially diametrically opposed to each other, yet in many ways their substance and rhetoric were surprisingly similar (Arendt, 1951). This seems helpful and important for making sense of ideologies more generally. Thus, as well as having their own inherent interest, they offer more far-reaching insights for attempting to understand political ideology.

The hatred of their instigators for each other was not only reflected in the brutality of the conflict between Nazi Germany and the Soviet Union, but also the extreme violence that took place between German communists and Nazis (the most powerful and developed expression of fascism) between the wars. This was also reflected in the horrors associated with the Spanish Civil War. Yet these ideologies expressed shared commitment to the wellbeing of their peoples as a primary goal. Thus for Lenin, founder of the Soviet Union, the dictatorship of the proletariat would 'transform their productive relations so that, in the long run … genuine social freedom [would be] realised' (Harding, 1996, p 159). The Nazis stressed that Germany must honour its workers and there was a preoccupation with protecting German people from economic, social and other threats. Both were also determinedly international movements (Fritzsche, 1990 p 45; Tooze, 2006, p 37).

The regimes advancing these ideologies were totalitarian in nature, effectively controlled by dictatorships, offering their populations little if any say or control. In both cases, their subjects not only had to accede to their control, but also seemed to have to internalise it. Both imposed the most extreme punishments on dissidents and both saw the rights and interests of the individual as subordinate to those of the party/collectivity/state. Each had its own 'out groups'; those of the Soviet Union's founders were peasants and the 'lumpen-proletariat' – the poorest most insecure people at the bottom of the economic ladder; those of the Nazis, freemasons, gay and disabled people, Jews, gypsies and others seen as racially inferior.

All this raises two questions for this book's discussion. First, given that most people had so little say or control over either of these political ideologies, how did they manage to enlist so much support, so that tens of millions would suffer and die for them? Second, with so many apparent similarities between the two ideologies, at least at an abstract and idealised level, how did each manage to generate so much hatred among so many people for the other?

We are hardly the first to ask these questions. For example, in the 1930s show trials, when Bolshevik leaders of the Russian Revolution confessed to anti-state crimes that they hadn't committed, it has been suggested that in some cases, as well as resulting from torture and threats, victims made such false confessions 'as a last service to the party' (Koestler, 1980).

The Left-winger George Orwell was one of the most important and high profile British commentators on political ideologies during the 1930s and 1940s. Unlike most commentators he was critical of both communist and fascist ideologies. This was particularly reflected in his account of his experience fighting in the Spanish Civil War, *Homage To Catalonia* (Orwell, 1938). Unlike many who supported the anti-fascist republican cause, he hadn't joined the Soviet supported International Brigade, but enlisted in the independent socialist POUM militia. This was to be attacked and suppressed by the Stalinist communists, its ostensible allies in the struggle against Franco. In his later books *Animal Farm* and *Nineteen Eighty-Four* (Orwell, 1945; 1949), he highlighted the way in which such totalitarian regimes not only demanded that the populace conformed to their demands but also were required to *believe in* them.

With so many things in common, with the mass of their supporters equally powerless to exert influence either over their authority or their own lives, you might wonder how these two political ideologies managed to set so many tens of millions at each other's throats. But they certainly were able to do just that. Authors like Arendt have highlighted the role of indoctrination and propaganda, between which she draws a distinction, in making this possible (Arendt, 1951, pp 343–4). Both these political ideologies and their leaders were highly skilled at manipulating people. As Ian Kershaw the historian noted of the Nazis:

> The repeated claim before the 'seizure of power' – that the NSDAP [Nazi Party], as a national social-revolutionary movement, and not simply another political party ... would create new bonds of unity through its elimination and transcending of the party system, was highly attractive and conveyed much of Nazism's dynamic appeal. (Kershaw, 1987, p 103)

A direct quote from Joseph Stalin himself makes the same point:

> It is difficult for me to imagine what 'personal liberty' is enjoyed by an unemployed hungry person. True freedom can only be where there is no exploitation and oppression of one person by another; where there is not unemployment, and where a person is not living in fear of losing his job, his home and his bread. Only in such a society personal and any other freedom can exist for real and not on paper. (Stalin, undated)

This last from a paranoid tyrant who allowed no dissent or challenge that he saw as potentially threatening to himself. And this really seems to be the point. What it really tells us is that ideologies may be absolutely out of our control; that we may nonetheless believe in them and, that many of us also may suffer or die for them – willingly or not. While the masters of competing political ideologies recruit the rest of us to fight their wars, ultimately their conflicts may only be a form of shadow boxing to keep them in power and subordinate the rest of us. This argument was of course most developed in George Orwell's dystopian novel *Nineteen Eighty-Four* (Orwell, 1949). Here the perpetual conflicts and ever changing alliances between Oceania, Eurasia and Eastasia primarily serve the purpose of using up resources and keeping populations in line. And still we seem to support, or at least acquiesce to, such political ideologies. This is a further measure of the power and regressive potential of ideologies given force at the most extreme level – and of the importance of trying to untangle the conundrums they set us more generally.

3

Imposing ideology

If you're not careful, the newspapers will have you hating the people who are being oppressed, and loving the people who are doing the oppressing.

Malcolm X, African-American leader

If the premise of this book is correct and few of us have much say or involvement in the ideologies that most affect us, what does shape and give them power? To recap, let's check what we have been finding out about ideology so far. A political ideology is a set of values and ideas. But these are not neutral and they have to have power behind them to have any effect. We all of us may have our own personal ideology or set of such values and goals, but unless we are able to share or impose them on other people, they have little or no meaning or significance beyond us. They may just influence our internal lives and the lives of those close to us. An ideology may guide where we are going or it may be used to justify where we are being taken. While the 20th century saw the emergence of new ideologies like fascism and communism whose reverberations still affect our lives today, the ideology that most of us live under – and that means most of us in the world – is neoliberalism. Neoliberalism refers to the resurgence from the late 20th century of 19th century liberal ideas associated with free-for-all market economics and the devaluing of state intervention to help people.

Different ideological perspectives are used by humans to explain, justify or legitimise a political or social order. Ideology can be and often is used to justify oppression. It does not oppress in itself. Ideology is *used* to do so. And it tends to be used by one group of people – generally a more powerful group of people – against other less powerful groups. A variety of means and techniques are used to advance such political ideologies. It is these we want to turn to now to get a clearer idea of the pressures operating on people to adopt any political ideology and indeed to choose a particular one. These include:

- force
- education
- mass media
- language

- arts and culture
- propaganda
- knowledge claims
- internalisation

(Freeman, 2003; Hoffman and Graham, 2006)

It is important to remember that ideological preferences are unlikely to be shaped by just one of these potential drivers. They are likely instead to work in various and complex ways together (Feldman and Johnston, 2013). First, let's look a little closer at these possible powers behind political ideology.

Force

As the last chapter showed, the most obvious and unambiguous way in which ideologies are imposed is through *force*. This can be achieved by using military and security forces to maintain internal control. But it is also achieved through denial of individual and collective rights, through control of the judiciary and access to justice, and the threat of the penal system, imprisonment, torture and death. These are the blunt instruments for imposing ideologies, but there are other less obvious but no less effective methods, all of which have played key roles in the modern history of political ideologies, from China through to the former East Germany. We should also remember that force can operate in more and less subtle ways in 'western democracies', as the Black Lives Matter movement highlights.

Education

Our lives and outlook are shaped by our *socialisation*; that is, what we learn and internalise about ourselves, the world we live in and our relationships with it, from babyhood through our formative years. This is in part shaped by those who bring us up and who constitute our 'important others'. This includes our family, friends and loved ones. But it is also crucially influenced by our formal education. That is why in modern public policy, education has always been seen as particularly central to the achievement of greater equality and social justice (Karabel and Halsey, 1977). The impact of education extends beyond what we are actually taught, to the values, assumptions and ideas that underpin this; also to the role models and relationships that we learn of as valued and devalued. Schools are often the first external society we join and there we are subjected to some of our most important lessons beyond the curriculum – how to be boys and girls, men and women, about diversity and equality, and about our relationships, not least with the state. Schools are inseparable from ideological ambitions. If parents pay for their children to go to public schools to gain confidence, status, networks and to question, the compulsory UK state system has more often been concerned with ensuring conformity and people's preparation for the labour market.

Mass media

The role of mass media as handmaiden, transmitter and amplifier of ruling ideologies has long been recognised and highlighted. This can range from regime-controlled media strictly advancing the party line, to subtler arrangements between governments and ostensibly independent media like those in the UK, for example, between the Conservative Party, political Right and the *Daily Mail*, *Sun*, *Times* and *Telegraph*. Whichever it is, the media are used to reinforce the prevailing view of the world and the regime advancing it (Croteau and Hoynes, 2018, pp 107–50). It is not only in relation to war that 'truth is the first casualty', as the Greek dramatist Aeschylus wrote two and a half millennia ago. In the US we have seen former President Trump dismiss non-compliant media as purveyors of 'fake news' (Woodward, 2018). Following his unexpected success in the 2017 UK general election, Labour leader Jeremy Corbyn was demonised by Right-wing media variously for being a Marxist, wearing unfashionable clothes and appealing to young people.

President Trump's meretricious talk of 'fake news' called into question mainstream news services, but all news is manufactured, whether print, broadcast or internet based. This is so in the sense that it is selected, interpreted and prioritised according to a complex process of media and ruling values and processes and negotiation between news creators (organisations, individuals and publicising institutions) and news transmitters (mass media). Anyone who has tried to gain visibility for a cause, product or pop star knows this only too well (Beresford, 1979).

There is no doubt that mass media are able to exert a major influence on the public expression of social attitudes. The high level vilification of immigrants and people receiving welfare benefits in the UK that intensified in the early 21st century has little to do with any objective truth or reality. Instead, it can be traced to determined concerted attacks on them by Right-wing politicians and fellow-travelling mass media (Ryan, 2019).

Propaganda

Overlapping with mass media is propaganda; that is, deliberate misinformation spread by leaders, states, governments and their allies to counter what is actually happening and/or manipulate support for them. The philosopher Hannah Arendt drew a distinction between such *propaganda*, whose aim in totalitarian regimes she believed was to persuade the outside world, and *indoctrination*, whose purpose was to keep government supporters on side (Arendt, 1951, p 343). Propaganda also overlaps with culture more broadly as developed in the new Soviet Union as 'agitprop' after the Russian Revolution. This was spread to the public through popular media, including art, theatrical performance and film (Smith, 1989, p 124).

Language

Related to this, language is also used as a key tool to serve the interests of ideologies and the goals their advocates pursue (Ghaderinezhad, 2015). In an age of mass industrialised killing, warfare is presented in individualising, romanticised terms of 'heroes', hardware and commemoration to disguise its awful meanings and consequences. New words are invented to hide the reality of policies and politics that are against most people's interests or which are intended to divide and rule, for example, 'collateral damage', 'smart bombs', 'nudge' and 'trickle down economics', 'asylum seekers' (as opposed to refugees, when originally the term refugee meant seeking refuge/asylum), 'hard working families' (you, as opposed to people on benefits) and so on.

It was George Orwell, the 20th century writer and commentator we encountered in the previous chapter, who most developed critical thinking about the use of language by ruling ideologies, especially totalitarian states. Language is used ideologically to guide us to think in the way it wants us to. As he highlighted with the language 'Newspeak' he developed in his novel *Nineteen Eighty-Four*, language can limit and control our thoughts, ideas and understandings (Orwell, 1949). If Orwell was influenced by developments in Stalin's Soviet Russia and the international communist party, much more of what he described has since come to pass, in societies that see themselves as liberal democracies as well as those typified as tyrannies.

Arts and culture

Most of us are familiar with the idea of propaganda, as information used – indeed often misused – for ideological purposes. But we also tend to draw a distinction between such propaganda and arts and culture more generally. In fact, arts and culture tend at least to reflect dominant ideologies and at most to advance their structures and purposes, however questionable these may be. Arts and culture are not only a vehicle for transmitting and reinforcing political ideology, they are also majorly shaped by it (Croteau and Hoynes, 2018, pp 107–50). Britain's class-ridden dominant arts and culture is still overshadowed by the racism, colonialism, sexism, heterosexism and disablism that new social movements have targeted for close on half a century. As we have seen, it has taken Hollywood more than a century even to expose the sexual harassment of women that has long been trivialised as 'casting couch' culture and which still signifies the personal, social and economic subordination of women.

It is not just in *Nineteen Eighty-Four*'s Oceania that history is rewritten. We watch it on primetime television as the gross inequalities of Edwardian Britain are rewritten as a saga of compassionate class relations – *Downton Abbey* – from the pen of Tory peer Julian Fellowes. Similarly, we are fed back to ourselves on 'reality television' as caricatures privileging ruling neoliberal preoccupations with celebrity, wealth and consumerist individualism. Arts and culture are subtle and highly effective ideological weapons. It's not surprising that they were so highly valued and developed, for example, in the forms of radio, film, mass display and festivals (Thompson, 2016), in the defining tyrannies of the 20th century, Nazi Germany, militarist Japan, Soviet Russia, Maoist China and Kim family North Korea.

Knowledge claims

Ideologies are grounded in knowledge claims. That is, their proponents make claim to knowledge that supports and justifies their view of the world and their part in it. These knowledge claims are presented as having authority, and much power may be attached to them. Knowledge and power are key interconnected components of ideology. Such knowledge claims tend to be offered as truths, backed up by science, rather than being based on values and assumptions (Lynch, 1994; Eagleton, 1994; Morris, 2016). They are also often presented as if the knowledge they rest on belongs to all of us, when in fact it can often truly only be claimed by the small group that has ownership of the ideology. Thus the knowledge claims of past ideologies that:

- human beings are born equal
- human freedom is pivotally important
- capital is at the heart of everything

Thus, also the founding liberal position on the 'social contract', which asserts that the individual consents to be governed by the state on the basis of its recognition of their equality and protection of their individual rights. We may wonder how many agricultural and industrial labourers who were contemporaries of the political philosopher John Locke, who advanced this knowledge claim, would have experienced their life in this way (Huemer, 2012). More recently, Thatcherism has been based on a rejection of state intervention and prioritising of the market, deregulation and the private sector as a creator of wealth. As progressive social mobility has declined and poverty, housing problems and inequality greatly increased, again we may wonder how convincing this claim looks to growing numbers of people at or below the average wage or without access to owner occupation in higher price housing areas.

The idea of 'ideology' is itself a product of the 'Age of Reason' and 'the Enlightenment', with their preoccupation with experiment and 'science'. Significantly, the key political ideologies of modernism have all based their knowledge claims on 'science' and being scientific. Whatever we think of these claims and their 'science' or pseudo-science, they have had enormous power and impacted on hundreds of millions of people. For example:

- the Nazis and their racial theory of Aryanism;
- Lenin's and Stalin's Soviet Union and Lysenkoism and historical materialism;
- Maoist China's related policy of agricultural collectivisation;
- the political new Right and the economics of Friedrich Hayek (Josephson, 2005).

Ideologies develop their own founding myths, histories, explanations and knowledge. Acceptance of these is likely to be part and parcel of living under such ideologies. Questioning or rejection of such knowledge claims are unlikely to be welcomed and in totalitarian regimes can be expected to have very negative consequences, as a challenge to that regime and its legitimacy.

Internalisation

However, it is important to stress that ideologies are not only imposed from without. They are developed to bring about change and conformity within us. As Inner Party member O'Brien says to Winston Smith in *Nineteen Eighty-Four*: 'We do not destroy the heretic because he resists us ... We convert him, we capture his inner mind, we reshape him. We burn all evil and all illusion out of him; we bring him over to our side, not in appearance, but genuinely, heart and soul' (Orwell, 1949).

All of the techniques and methods we have identified which are used to advance ideological perspectives are also used to bring about internal change within us, to change our minds, to influence our attitudes, to secure our agreement, support and acquiescence (Eagleton, 1991, pp 1–40). Thus it is that we often see the supporters of fiercely conflicting ideologies, who may actually have much in common, engaged in the large-scale killing of each other, while the architects of such opposed ideologies have much more in common with one other and are more likely to die in their beds.

No wonder there are jokes about 'turkeys voting for Christmas' when Right-wing political parties with billionaire leaders and sponsors and overt policies of regressive redistribution win popular votes. No wonder the increasing interest in 'populist' politics when neoliberal politicians like Silvio Berlusconi, Donald Trump and Boris Johnson secure widespread support from working-class voters and those who see themselves as dispossessed (Wodak, 2015). It doesn't seem to be enough for the proponents of ideologies to force us to accept them. They want us to be genuinely committed to and believe in them. And they seem to have developed new psychologically based electioneering methods which help ensure this happens, as was seen in the UK with both the 2016 Brexit referendum and the general election result of 2019 (Beresford, 2020).

It is because of this that thinkers like the Italian Marxist politician and philosopher Antonio Gramsci (1891–1937) continue to be seen as having relevance and importance. Gramsci developed the theory of 'cultural hegemony' or dominance. He described how the state and ruling class used cultural institutions to maintain power in capitalist societies rather than simply violence or coercion. A 'hegemonic culture propagates its own values and norms so that they become the "commonsense" values of all and maintain the status quo' (Jackson Lears, 1985 Eagleton, 2007, pp 93–125). Thus capitalist societies enlist people's agency and active support rather than simply imposing structural constraints and enforcing their compliance.

The pragmatism of ideological positions

As we have seen, ideologies and ideological perspectives are presented as an *end* in their own right: that is to say, they embrace and point us to particular goals and values. However, they can also be seen as a *means* to an end – and not only as offering ways of achieving their explicit ends. They may be used to offer ways of buttressing the power of their proponents: that is to say they are ultimately concerned with safeguarding the latter's interests. As a result they tend to be used pragmatically. This does not mean that they are necessarily responsive to their critics or external attacks, or that they are readily open to popular change, but rather that we may expect enduring ideologies to bend with the times.

Thus despite the essential atheism of Soviet communism, Stalin reopened the churches and reinstated God to help unify the population against the wartime Nazi threat. Hitler declared the Japanese 'honorary Aryans' to enlist them on his side in the Second World War. The UK Conservative Party passed the notorious Section 28 of the 1988 Local Government Act stating that councils should not 'intentionally promote homosexuality or publish material with the intention of promoting homosexuality' in their schools or other areas of their work. Twenty-five years later, however, it was a Conservative-led coalition which set in train legislation for same-sex marriage in Great Britain (but not Northern Ireland) and appointed an out lesbian leader in Scotland in 2011.

The ownership of political ideologies

Two strong themes have so far emerged in this discussion. The first is that the idea and reality of ideologies do not seem to be things that are common currency for many of us. We haven't necessarily had the chance to investigate the idea or make sense of the practice. Ideological perspectives may be at the heart of our school learning, with, for example, endless examination of the Nazi regime and the Second World War in the UK national curriculum. But this does not mean that we are helped to critique ideological issues or the ideologies operating on us – from our schooling onwards.

Second, we have learnt that political ideologies are the set of principles, values and ideas advanced by a group, class or movement to explain how society should work and which set out a political and cultural blueprint for a particular social order. This has been the history of the development of the idea of ideology since the term was first formulated during the French Revolution. Political ideologies follow from the goals and aspirations of leaders, vanguards, privileged intellectuals and other elites. So far we have found nothing to contradict this generalisation. They are not the result of democratic processes of development. Most people who are the subject of a political ideology have little or no say in it. This is hardly remarkable, except in its implications. The political process for most of us is at best an indirect one, where we entrust our political rights to another through how we cast a vote. This is the best most of us can hope for, who do not have opportunities to exert influence through particular personal, status or financial power.

These two preconditions set up a perfect storm for the perpetuation of ideologies over which most of us have no control. Not only are we unlikely to have any say or control over ideologies affecting us, we may not even realise this or recognise it as an issue. As the cultural historian Morris Berman put it: 'An idea is something you have; an ideology is something that has you' (Berman, 2001, page not known). For most of us, the ideologies we live under are the taken-for-granted context of our lives, the boundaries and furniture with which we live. We may do this more or less consciously, with more or less understanding. Insofar as people are aware of them, we would suggest that most people tacitly accept the ideologies operating on them – if they even appreciate these are at work. Ownership or the lack of it is not even something that tends to be seen as problematic. Most of us are certainly unlikely to assume we have or should have any say in such established ideologies. This itself presumes a familiarity and understanding of ideas and structures of ideology that cannot be taken for granted.

We may be encouraged to have the sense of exercising choice and control within the parameters of ruling ideologies, for instance, through the ballot box in Western democracies, but this is not the same thing. The key ideology that most of us – and that means most of us in the world – live under, as stated earlier, is neoliberalism. It would be simplistic to equate Western democratic ideologies with totalitarian ones – the former at least offer us formal political rights – but it would also be mistaken to assume that we all necessarily have some meaningful control over such political ideologies. While ideologies like Western liberal democracy may be formally framed in participative, democratic terms, the reality is not only that we are not all politically equal under the law, but we all of us have greatly differing degrees of say over such ideological positions. Powerful elites may have a significant influence over them, but this does not hold for most of us. So what do we do about this? That is the focus of the next step in our discussion.

Challenging dominant ideologies: the crucial contradiction

This book has stressed that most of us are unlikely to challenge the political ideologies that impact on our lives. This may be because we don't think to, don't want to, don't dare to – or don't even realise we could. But that isn't true for everyone. There are always rebels, dissenters and dissidents, who reject the ideas and values imposed upon them and seek something else.

That search is unlikely to go unrewarded. Unless we have the misfortune to live in a totalitarian police state – and even then, digging tends to unearth all kinds of covert rebellious thought and action – there is unlikely to be any shortage of alternatives on offer. We can expect to encounter groupings, organisations, oppositions and parties of every imaginable ideological colour, ranging from the hardest Left and Right, including some which refuse to be categorised in terms of the conventional Left-Right political spectrum. Some we may see as coming within dominant ideology, while others reject this or key aspects of it. Sometimes such initiatives come to fruition in the fall of governments. They may also result in coup d'états, revolts, revolutions, insurrections, mutinies and assassinations.

Any more participatory?

We can make our choice about giving our allegiance to an alternative ideology, subject of course to our own socialisation, idiosyncrasies, preferences, awareness, predilections and pressures. But this may well be the *only* choice we can make in the matter. However big or small, powerful or powerless the party or grouping we choose from, the likelihood is that we will not have much say in its ideological offering. Indeed, we would suggest most of us are likely to have as little say in it as the most enthusiastic supporter of a UK Premier League football team does in their club. Even where we are seeking to reject an ideological position and exert control over another adopted position, we may still have little say and must take what is given us, rather than play a part in shaping it.

The French philosopher and writer Albert Camus made this point in 1951 in his book *The Rebel* when he wrote: 'Methods of thought which claim to give the lead to our world in the name of revolution have become, in reality, ideologies of consent and not of rebellion' (Camus, 2000, page not known). But this was not a new idea, even then. Individuals with an interest in political ideology as far apart as Napoleon Bonaparte and George Orwell have highlighted that those who may be dissatisfied with prevailing political ideologies may be no more interested in advancing a less oppressive, more liberatory alternative – or in working towards it with others in a democratic way.

> Among those who dislike oppression are many who like to oppress. (Bonaparte, undated)

> No one believes more firmly than Comrade Napoleon that all animals are equal. He would be only too happy to let you make your decisions for yourselves. But sometimes you might make the wrong decisions, comrades, and then where should we be? (Orwell, 1945, chapter 5)

The lesson to be learned here is that those who seek to challenge ruling ideologies aren't necessarily interested in challenging the non-participative ways in which they are developed, imposed and perpetuated. Consequently, those who sign up to them may find that there is no greater commitment to participation among their initiators than was the case with the political ideology they seek to challenge and displace. This does not mean that all such ideologies are reactionary and destructive. Clearly the redistributive ideology underpinning the post-war UK welfare state cannot be seen as perpetuating the same inequalities and exclusions as its poor law predecessor. But, as we shall see later, the top-down way in which it was created also contained the seeds of its own destruction (Beresford, 2016).

Exceptions to the rule

There may be exceptions to this rule of course, where ideologies not only proclaim participation but also embody the aspiration to participation in their construction and development. Anarchism is the obvious and self-conscious one. Anarchism is a political philosophy that advocates self-governing societies, based on non-hierarchical and free associations and a rejection of the state (Franks, 2013). 'Anarchism does not offer a fixed body of doctrine from a single particular world view, instead fluxing and flowing as a philosophy' (Marshall, 1993, pp 14–17; Kropotkin, 2020). Some commentators have suggested that the modern Occupy movement has roots in anarchism, although others reject this. Occupy is a socio-political movement against inequality, seeking to advance social and economic justice and new forms of democracy (Gibson, 2013).

Similarly, the kind of socialism which Robert Tressell advocated in *The Ragged Trousered Philanthropists* (first published in 1914) highlighted the collective efforts of workers and opposition to capitalism (Tressell, 2004). But we never learn from Tressell how 'the glorious fabric of the Co-operative Commonwealth' he hoped for and envisaged was actually to come about or how his 'risen sun of Socialism' was to be shaped and maintained by its intended beneficiaries. Little is said about the *process*, as if it would find its own natural expression. But the history of both socialism and communism has highlighted that much more than that hope is likely to be needed if it is not to be appropriated by a particular interest, faction or elite, or if the structures for managing it are not to become excluding institutions in their own right. Similar criticisms are made about the practicality of anarchism, although we have seen its flowering, for example, in Catalonia, before it was destroyed by Franco and the nationalists in the Spanish Civil War (Orwell, 1938).

The ideological merry-go-round

There is an irony here, one which rarely seems to be discussed. We would argue that this is a key issue and therefore we want to highlight it.

> This is that the purveyors of oppositional ideology may offer
> us no more say and control over that ideological perspective
> as have those they are seeking to challenge and supplant.

Perhaps more to the point this often does not even seem to be an issue in dispute. Instead it can feel much more taken for granted. Yet we know from many examples in history that once a system has been established, the same ideology that challenged the status quo can then be used to maintain it.

Meanwhile, our role can end up merely as one of foot soldiers for other people's ideological positions and causes; the stage army that gives them an appearance of popular support and democratic control. We are expected to attend a party's or grouping's meetings, sell its publications, and canvass for more supporters like ourselves. In due course, we are signed up to and probably internalise *its* ideological position, as we pay our subscriptions, serve our apprenticeship and demonstrate our commitment.

It is not difficult to see the consequences of this from our ordinary experience. Over the years, women and people from Black and minority ethnic communities have supported the values of oppositional parties and trade unions in societies like the UK in order to achieve equal rights and opportunities. Yet for many years those organisations have conspicuously failed to treat women and Black and minority ethnic people with equality. So, after the Second World War when opportunities and responsibilities for both (overlapping) groups had expanded massively, the Labour Party and trade unions supported the enforced return of women to the home and restricted immigration to protect the male labour force, despite their stated allegiance to equality (Beresford, 2016).

We would also argue that this lack of say in oppositional ideologies is as true of those associated with a revolutionary approach to opposition and change as it is those associated with parliamentary or gradualist approaches. Whatever the particular ideological position embraced by revolutionaries, what can usually be said is that if they are successful, there continues to be a dominant or elite group and all that tends to change is who or what makes up that group. Whether we are talking about the economic class conflict of Marx or the permanent revolution of Trotsky or the Chilean neoliberalism of General Pinochet, what we tend to see is that rulers continue to rule and that unequal and hierarchical social relations continue to operate.

Our only way to exert influence may be to become like one of the People's Front of Judea's 'splitters' that we shall be hearing from in the next section, atomising into ever more fragmented and individualised ideological positions. And, of course, as we are also told that 'unity is strength', the more we divide ourselves, the weaker these are likely to become. Interestingly, while the talk in political and social movements is more often about leadership and developing leadership roles, for most of us the role we can expect to be positioned in is as a *follower*. Yet there is hardly the same discussion about 'followership', as there is about leadership.

It was this desire to unify the emergent feminist movement and socialist politics in the 1970s which gave rise to the Beyond The Fragments movement, but while this achieved prominence and significance, it was unable to transcend existing divisions, unify or democratise leftist politics (Rowbotham et al, 1979; 2013).

So whether we are talking about dominant or oppositional ideologies, however liberatory these are presented as, ownership generally seems to be narrowly based. While they may change over time and be open to some influence, this certainly does not mean that they are socially constructed in any democratic sense. How might we change this – how might we have more emancipatory ideology? This is the key question for this discussion. This is what we want to begin to examine in the next section.

Ruled and divided

People continually hive off oppositional ideologies as they find existing ones inadequate and/or unresponsive to their attempts to influence them. This has perhaps been most powerfully and popularly illustrated in the Monty Python film, *Life of Brian*, in the sketch which touches on Judean resistance to Roman occupation. While this may seem a strange reference to bring into a challenging discussion of political ideology, it uniquely and explicitly makes the point, made much more seriously in the feminist text *Beyond The Fragments* around the same time (Rowbotham et al, 1979). Externally imposed ideological positions can be the most obvious enemy of solidarity and unity. We frequently seem to have to fit into them rather than shape them ourselves as an alternative to the status quo. Monty Python must be one of the few instances where a critique of the divisiveness of radical political ideology has become a high profile part of comedic popular culture.

BRIAN:	Are you the Judean People's Front?
REG:	Fuck off!
BRIAN:	What?
REG:	Judean People's Front. We're the People's Front of Judea! Judean People's Front. Cawk.
FRANCIS:	Wankers.
BRIAN:	Can I ... join your group?
REG:	Listen. If you wanted to join the P.F.J. (People's Front of Judea), you'd have to really hate the Romans.
BRIAN:	I do!
REG:	Oh, yeah? How much?
BRIAN:	A lot!
REG:	Right. You're in. Listen. The only people we hate more than the Romans are the fucking Judean People's Front.
P.F.J.:	Yeah ...
JUDITH:	Splitters.
P.F.J.:	Splitters ...
FRANCIS:	And the Judean Popular People's Front.

P.F.J.:   Yeah. Oh, yeah. Splitters. Splitters …
LORETTA: And the People's Front of Judea.
P.F.J.:   Yeah. Splitters. Splitters …
REG: What?
LORETTA: The People's Front of Judea. Splitters.
REG: We're the People's Front of Judea!
LORETTA: Oh. I thought we were the Popular Front.
REG: People's Front! C–huh.
FRANCIS: Whatever happened to the Popular Front, Reg?
REG: He's over there.
P.F.J.:   Splitter!
               (Another Bleedin Monty Python website, undated)

Of course, this also raises the issue of how far participatory approaches to developing ideology could actually accommodate differences of opinion. This is a big issue which is examined in more detail in the third part of the book. But next we come to Part II.

PART II

Reclaiming participation

4

A different approach to ideology

> The master's tools will never dismantle the master's house.
> Audre Lorde, African-American feminist, 2007

Here in the second part of the book, we begin its central task, reconnecting ideology and participation. Most of us are likely to prefer life under a political ideology that values and respects us. However, as we have seen, we are more likely to live under value systems that do the opposite – except for the elites who control them. Yet often we end up as cheerleaders for them. The images that we remember, whether of Donald Trump's first presidential election campaign or Adolf Hitler's endless Nazi party gatherings, are of huge cheering crowds, not the billionaires and large corporations that quietly bankrolled them and which most profited from their victories and who tend to die peacefully in their beds. So how do we escape this enduring contradiction?

First, let's try and untangle what we seem to be learning so far about ideologies. Different ideological perspectives are used by humans to explain, justify or legitimise a political or social order. In this way, ideology may be used to justify oppression, even though it does not oppress in itself. Ideologies are of course closely linked with power. They are used to justify the distribution of power in society.

Ideologies often have a lot to say about freedom and equality. Yet they rarely seem to be constructed or developed in a participatory or democratic way in keeping with such values. This is inherently problematic. It means that in their making they are unlikely to reflect and include everyone's interests, experience, knowledge and perspectives. How then, if that is the case, will they adequately reflect and address everyone's rights, responsibilities and entitlements? We might expect that they would inevitably privilege some at the expense of others, and that is what tends to happen; they reflect ruling cultural, social and political hierarchies – and it is these which tend to shape them.

The paradox that has already begun to emerge in this text is that revolutionaries and reformers frequently seem to seek progressive change through methods that are as exclusionary and narrowly based as those they aim to displace. Not surprisingly, the outcomes are often counterproductive. Even if this point has not featured centrally in ideological discussion, it has been made by some activists and thinkers conscious of the reality that we are unlikely to remake our world in a different more equal image if we rely on the same old exclusionary and unequal processes. As the gay civil rights activist Bayard Rustin summed it up:

> [We] must remember that we cannot hope to achieve democracy and equality in such a way that would destroy the very kind of society which we hope to build. If we desire a society of peace, then we cannot achieve such a society through violence. If we desire a society without discrimination, then we must not discriminate against anyone in the process of building this society. If we desire a society that is democratic, then democracy must become a means as well as an end. (Rustin, 1969)

Thus there is an important distinction to be made. If we are saying we need participatory ideologies, then we are saying more than that a participatory ideology is one committed to freedom and equality, or to the more equal distribution of power in society, or that a participatory ideology equals a system of ideas and values about how to have a political/social order that promotes equality and freedom.

Instead we are arguing for something different and much more. We are arguing that the only way to develop ideas about how to promote equality and freedom is to develop those ideas *together on equal terms*. To achieve such an outcome, we must use the same method – that is, inclusive democratic participation. This is the point made perhaps most famously by Audre Lorde and repeated at the top of this chapter (Lorde, 2007).

While people and parties who want to impose ideologies upon us may continue to do so, if we want to advance truly liberatory ideologies to challenge that, then we will need to do things differently. This is the key and vital lesson we are faced with. But this means change in everything: in our selves, our institutions, our assumptions, power and responsibility. Initially this may seem like an awesome undertaking. But little else seems to work. And what we must also remind ourselves is that so much work has already been done, if we are prepared to stand on the shoulders of the giants who have done it, rather than disregard their pioneering work. We do not start from a blank page. This is a task that must be restarted, augmented and continued.

Participation: a paradigm change

There is much to build on. But we must constantly remember that we are talking here about a step change in how we do things. It can be difficult to break old habits. Those of us used to leadership roles tend to import them unconsciously into efforts to involve or democratise. Those of us more used to doing what we are told in an increasingly hierarchical world can make that even easier for those at the top of the tree by falling into traditional subordinate, follower roles. Many approaches to participatory democracy fail – because they are not participatory in their process.

Thus the prevailing approaches to participatory democracy, like 'deliberative democracy', tend to be heavily structured. Citizens' juries, citizens' assemblies and local referenda, for example, are imposed top down, shaped by prevailing agendas and draw in a very limited range of participants – the more advantaged, confident and assertive people – who generally tend to get involved (Street et al, 2014).

Opening up the discussion

So, if we want to develop and live under democratic and emancipatory ideologies, then we have to struggle to achieve them in democratic, inclusive and emancipatory ways. We need first to recognise this as an issue and then work out how to take it forward.

The crucial first step must be to try to open up the discussion. It's hardly likely to be a very inclusive discussion at present when ideology, as we have already seen, is a word and idea that few people feel comfortable with and many are worried or frightened by. So we must go back a few steps, stop taking things for granted. We must stop assuming that people know what we are talking about and make it more possible for them to be part of the conversation on more equal terms.

We need to become aware of these exclusions, think them through and also work to recognise ways in which we may either be excluded or particularly privileged and advantaged, since both can have damaging consequences.

These exclusions have implications for everything that relates to politics, ideologies and political change:

- how we develop discussion
- learning and education
- knowledge formation and research

- how people are involved
- how decisions are made
- how we organise, work and do things together
- how we develop ideas
- speaking for ourselves
- how we judge or evaluate success

Where this discussion now stands

This author, of course, recognises that not everyone will share his commitment to equality and social justice and that not all political ideologies are signed up to these values. This is the reality and it is not disputed. But many *are* signed up and here the argument is that there is an inherent problem and contradiction when ideologies committed to democratic values are not developed in participatory and democratic ways.

Of course, political ideologies offer different explanations for inequality. Some certainly are not based on advancing equality, but rather see inequality as a necessary or valued principle. Certainly Margaret Thatcher articulated this view, for example, in relation to educational mobility, income levels and life chances. Many clearly share her view. But this text is concerned with challenging inequality and social injustice. So its arguments are not focused on reactionary political ideologies; these certainly do not need broader involvement to maintain their position – although they may find themselves using populist and demagogic arguments to do so.

Critics may also suggest that the argument offered here for participatory approaches to political ideology is itself just one ideological position. This is obvious and true; this author would be the last to dispute or seek to conceal this. There is no intention in the present discussion to pretend that the position adopted here is any less ideologically based or normative than any other relating to ideology.

Ultimately, the argument for participation is a moral and ethical one. There are practical and philosophical arguments too, for example:

- We are likely to get better policy and services if the people they are intended for have some say in them – after all 'who knows better how the shoe fits than the person who wears it'.
- How can you defend your belief in *democracy* if it doesn't actually allow the people – the '*demos*' – to have a hand in it?

But the essential argument is a moral one so long as we believe that it is wrong to impose things on people without them having any say-so. This is in direct line from the anti-British slogan before the American Revolution: 'Taxation without representation is tyranny'. Or, as the US actor and filmmaker John Cusack put it: 'But, you know, I'm sorry, I think democracy requires participation. I mean, I don't want to proselytize but I do feel some sort of duty to participate in the process in some way other than just blindly [sic] getting behind a political party' (Cusack, undated).

But *two* key points are being made here. First, that ideologies should be developed in participatory ways because that is the right thing to do. Second, that if we say we want to advance an ideological approach/perspective that is committed to democratic principles and social justice, it is difficult to see how that can be achieved while wedded to a non-participatory approach to doing so. The first point is an ideological one. The second could be subjected to test.

What is being argued here is that some ideologies are likely to be qualified in their democratic and emancipatory potential because they are neither democratic nor emancipatory in their process. It may be argued that this could equally apply to the proposals being made here and their underlying ideology. However, this author would argue that he has arrived at these from years of being involved in community, disabled people's, service users' and survivors' organisations and movements, where the aim and actuality has been to co-construct political ideology together as those directly affected by it, having been historically at the mercy of others' prescriptions. So these proposals and arguments are the result of participatory processes; they do not just come out of the air or the personal predilections of the present author.

New social movements

Some of the most helpful insights that can be gained both about exclusions operating on political ideology and how they can be challenged have emerged from the 'new social movements' that emerged internationally in the latter part of the 20th century (which Audre Lorde was part of, for example) and it is these we need to turn to next.

It was the emergence of what have been called 'new social movements' in the latter part of the 20th century which first really highlighted the routine exclusions and discriminations that operate in societies beyond class differences and offered theories to understand them

(Buechler, 1999). These movements remind us all that great swathes of people were being left out or marginalised in political and other developments, including oppositional developments. They showed how many groups were spoken for, interpreted by and marginalised by prevailing institutions, interests and groups – often the very groups that they saw as their oppressors.

New social movements were characterised as different to *traditional* social movements because the focus of many was primarily on rights (gay rights, Black rights, animal rights, women's rights) rather than material economic wellbeing. Others were concerned with more recently identified issues, for example, environmentalism, peace and anti-nuclear power. Many of these movements related to identity and experience, movements for women, Black civil rights, disabled people, psychiatric system survivors, and lesbian, gay, bisexual, transgender and queer (LGBTQ) people. They also highlighted issues of 'intersectionality'; this recognises that identities are complex, interrelated and multifaceted, so that some people within some marginalised groups face particular discriminations and barriers. However, the ideas and insights from such viewpoints have often been ignored or devalued because of the crude tendency to treat difference hierarchically (Hill Collins and Bilge, 2016).

New social movements are particularly relevant here as they help make it possible to understand inequality as referring to more than poverty and other material inequalities. Now we can also more clearly see how inequality extends to the way in which the part some people and groups are able to play in the formation of discussion, policy, politics and indeed ideologies is especially limited. New social movements show us that such inequalities in involvement have to do with much more than traditionally understood differences in political power based on socio-economic status.

What distinguishes the movements based on identity is that they grew out of the sense of oppression and discrimination felt by the groups who established them. A number of social theorists identified the emergence in the late 20th century of a wide range of groups, which they conceived of as 'new social movements' (Touraine, 1981; Oliver, 1996). Characteristics associated by theorists with new social movements include that they:

- remain on the margin of the political system
- offer a critical evaluation of society
- imply a society with different forms of valuation and distribution

- raise issues which transcend national boundaries and they adopt an international perspective
    (Oliver, 1996, p 157; Oliver and Barnes, 2012, p 173)

Welfare user movements

The welfare service user movements, with which this author has long been involved, also connect with broader discussions about such new social movements. Between the late 1960s and 1980s a range of organisations and movements of welfare state service users emerged. A number of reasons for this development can be identified. These include people's dissatisfaction with the services and support they were receiving, a sense of injustice, a new assertiveness linked with more liberatory political times and the emergence of broader movements, as well as new political challenges to welfare states coming from both the political new Right and the radical Left (Campbell and Oliver, 1996). These movements included movements of disabled people, mental health service users/survivors, people with learning difficulties, looked after young people, older people and people living with HIV/AIDS. Such service users were associated with health, welfare and social care services. This was an international development. It took place both in advanced Western industrialised societies and also in the Global South/low-income countries. Local, regional, national, European and international organisations were established. The earliest established and best known of these movements is the disabled people's movement, which began to establish itself in the UK and internationally in the late 1960s and 1970s (Coleridge, 1993).

Such welfare service users experienced some of the most extreme exclusions, discrimination and oppression, for example, being institutionalised and denied citizen and human rights. The pioneering and innovative efforts of these movements to challenge such constraints are a key reason why they can be seen as fertile ground for gaining insights into both recognising and challenging the exclusionary nature of the development of ideologies. They reflect people's determined efforts to speak and act on their own behalf – to 'self-organise' – and to develop aims, ideas, ways of working and cultures of their own to achieve their own self-defined goals, rather than have others speak for them (Jordan and Lent, 1999; Lent, 2002). What unites welfare service user movements and many of the new social movements is that they are both based on identity and experience and people's efforts to define their own identities. They have all sought a revaluation of their social roles and worked to develop more positive identities.

This leads us next to some of the ways of challenging the exclusionary nature of many ideologies and much ideology formation. While there are many sources of insight for doing this, the service user movements already mentioned offer some of the most helpful and effective, and we will draw particularly on them.

Getting to grips with participation

It is becoming clear that if we want to advance more liberatory ideology then there will need to be a sea-change in how we seek to discuss and develop it. Key to this will be the idea of inclusive involvement – that is, the participation of those directly affected by political ideology in developing it.

To recap, we have interrogated the idea of 'ideology'. We have come to realise its importance and impact. We have considered its exclusionary nature and frequently destructive effects. We have argued the importance of people having a say in the ideologies that affect them and with which they align themselves. We have identified the importance of people's participation if we are to transform the ideologies that shape our lives and those of the worlds in which we live. We have begun to look at the international disabled people's movement as a case study of people working effectively to be involved and develop their own ideology – even if it is one that has come under constant attack and threat of subversion.

Unpacking participation

Starting with this first step, if we want to explore a more participatory approach to ideology more generally, then we need to pay as much attention to unpacking ideas and practices of *participation*, as we do to those of ideology. Participation is as complex, ambiguous and tricky an idea as ideology itself. We must avoid the mistake of trying to challenge traditional understandings of ideology by subjecting them to under-developed considerations of participation. This soon becomes apparent. We can quickly sense the importance of participation to committed activists. Thus the words of US radical and author Angela Davis: 'As a black woman, my politics and political affiliation are bound up with and flow from participation in my people's struggle for liberation, and with the fight of oppressed people all over the world against American imperialism' (Davis, 2018). Then we encounter the way would-be progressive politicians like Jeremy Corbyn, when seeking the leadership of the UK Labour Party, sought to acknowledge the centrality and value of such participation: 'I think we should talk about what the objectives of the party are, whether that's restoring the Clause Four as it was originally written or it's a different one, but I think we shouldn't shy away from public participation, public investment in industry, and public control of the railways' (Perraudin, 2015). However, it is not long before we also hear more cautious voices, like the US politician and sociologist Daniel Patrick Moynihan, warning us of the duplicitous and disempowering ways in which participation can be used: 'Citizen participation is a device whereby public officials induce non-public individuals to act in a way the officials desire' (Moynihan, undated).

Past history

Participation is an idea and term that has its own lengthy history, its own ideological relations and it lays many traps for those who don't treat it with care. If ideology is a word that can engender suspicion and hostility, participation in contrast is one that plays to people's hopes and susceptibilities. As has often been said, it is a 'feel-good' idea that can evoke a warm sense of togetherness, camaraderie and common cause. But, at the same time, participation is at the meeting point of the individual – as human being, citizen and social being – and political processes. This is a complex and difficult area. Here the private and public spheres in which we live our lives can collide. Here the inequalities that restrict some, notably women, to the private sphere, impact on people's opportunities to engage with the public sphere (Lister, 1991; 2003). This is vexed and contentious territory which human beings have sought to make sense of for millennia and where we can still routinely see some of the worst exclusions, discriminations and cruelties. That's why we want to make some effort here to treat this idea of 'participation' with the respect, caution and seriousness that it demands.

There is a tendency to treat ideas and practices of participation in isolation – as if they *don't* connect with broader political, ideological, social, cultural and human issues. For me, this is a fundamental error and problem. If we just see participation as some kind of gloss on existing structures, relations and systems of social organisation, then in my view we will never understand it or take it forward effectively. Put simply, participation isn't an add-on; some way of tweaking or adjusting existing arrangements, whatever those might be. So long as we accept this way of thinking, participation is unlikely to have any real meaning or make any real difference. Real participation changes *everything*.

Models and approaches

It all gets even more complicated when we try and establish what 'real participation' actually is. Over the years, numerous models and typologies for public participation have been developed. Perhaps the best known and most influential is Sherry Arnstein's 'ladder of citizen participation' in planning (Arnstein, 1969). This was set out as a linear progression from low to high participation. It ranged from non-participation at one end (manipulation and therapy), through tokenism (informing and consultation), to partnership and citizen control (categorised as citizen power). This 'eight step' model is helpful since it gives some conceptual clarity to the messy business of 'getting involved', highlighting the enormous range of intentions and outcomes that may be possible. However, as anyone who has long-term experience of trying to participate and have a say begins to appreciate, things can be expected to get much more complicated than this. As we might expect, participation is really much more complicated than a ladder and may not actually work in the linear way Arnstein suggested or only with the purposes she assumed (Collins and Ison, 2006).

When it comes to participation, intentions are not necessarily matched by results and agendas can be complex and, like the actors involved, multifaceted. From this activist's experience over many years, what is actually achieved by participation may not neatly correlate with where you are formally positioned on the ladder. Again from personal experience, honestly undertaken consultations may actually result in the achievement of more desired change than arrangements offered as co-production where inequalities of power inhibit what is actually possible.

The politics of participation

Perhaps most important, participation is not just a technical issue but also a political one. It is crucial not to consider it in isolation. Let's explain. Ancient Greece is seen as the birthplace of democracy and indeed of participation. The city state of Athens, which is most often identified as the cradle of democracy, had its own structures in place for direct or participatory democracy: citizens were directly involved in decision-making through a constant active process. But – and here is the big 'but' – only a minority of people, certainly no more than 10–20 per cent, counted as citizens and had a right to any say or involvement (Thorley, 2005; Raaflaub, 2007). We can still see who was excluded. In this system, you didn't count if you were a foreign resident or if you hadn't paid a debt. And of course you weren't part of the process if you were a slave – or even a freed slave. Just being the wrong kind of human being – that is, a woman – automatically counted you out. Only adult males who had completed their military training had the right to vote.

This is a very specific and limited meaning of 'participation'. And it was on a very small scale, so eminently manageable, at least in theory. Similarly, the history of participation since, despite much talk of 'popular movements' and 'grassroots action', is one that appears much more convincing from a distance than on close inspection. Like that other feel-good term 'community', attempts at participation are much more characterised by exclusions than inclusions.

Generally speaking, politics isn't popular and in the UK, for example, we don't really have a 'popular politics'. Yet ultimately, participation is very much a political concept. It is because of all these conflicts and contradictions that we need to deconstruct it very carefully and that is our next task.

First, as we have already suggested, public participation and participatory approaches are essentially ideological. We should stop there to signal the importance of this statement. If what we are saying is that the development of ideology needs to be participatory, we must be alert to a further layer of complexity here; that such participation is itself likely to be ideologically based. That means that it may be underpinned by very different aims and intentions. They are far from neutral technical exercises or ideas. Two ideologies have dominated recent discussion about public participation and 'user involvement'. These are probably best characterised as the 'consumerist/managerialist' approaches that have predominated under neoliberal/new Right politics and the democratic approaches of citizens, service users and new social movements (Winkler, 1987; Beresford and Croft, 1993a). With the first, the talk is of increasing the choice and control of the individual as a consumer, by seeking their input in policy and provision, through consultation and market research, in the same way that has long characterised efforts to maximise markets and consumption in private sector goods and services. The democratic approaches of service users, by contrast, are clearly concerned with participation that increases people's say and redistributes power to them so that they are able to achieve change through their involvement. This is the key concern of such approaches to involvement – being able to exert influence and make change.

It's also a reminder that participation can mean many different things, from having responsibility to having power, from being an unpaid volunteer to being an effective stakeholder in decision-making. And even when we are talking participation in the sense of being party to something, this can range from merely being present in a process, through expressing a view, to being able to make an effective difference. From the evidence it is clear that most people get involved in the hope of achieving the latter – having a say to be able to make change in line with their and others' preferences (Beresford and Croft, 1993a and 1993b; Beresford, 2016). It is not difficult to see that the supermarket model of participation outlined here, which conceives of people as consumers and is primarily concerned with increasing market share for providers of goods and services, has little in common with a democratic approach committed to bringing about social and personal change. As we have seen, whole typologies and scales of participation have been developed over the years to try to analyse the idea and help people make sense of and negotiate it effectively, yet still confusion about what is on offer, what is achievable, persists.

We should remember that participating does not necessarily mean having any say or control and it may serve the purposes of those who initiate it more than of those who respond to their invitations. The same terminology is often used to mean very different things. Thus in the context of international development, participation has also been identified as a means of denying and diverting people from effective say and control and can be used to oppress and control rather than liberate and empower (Cooke and Kothari, 2001; Hickey and Mohan, 2004).

We need to be clear what version of participation we are actually signing up to and what can be achieved by it. This isn't always the case and as a result people who get involved can often feel ignored, excluded or even abused. There is much talk of participation that is 'tokenistic' and which acts as a 'rubber stamp', where decisions have already been made before people have even had a chance to say what they think or where they just seem to be ignored if they disagree with the dominant viewpoint.

But, even where the aim is to achieve change and for people to be at the centre of things, the scenario may be more complex than first meets the eye. This is highlighted by the work of another major figure in the history of modern Western participation, Saul Alinsky. He was a community activist based in Chicago, author of *Rules For Radicals*, who focused on community organising and placed an emphasis on the role of the community organiser in community campaigning. Alinsky understood where many people were coming from, speaking of organising 'with people who do not participate in the endless responsibilities of citizenship and are resigned to live lives determined by others' (Alinsky, 1971). He understood the importance of appreciating their experience and paying attention to what they have to say.

Alinsky has been influential in community development work internationally since, including in the UK. But, as has been observed, he and many inspired by him placed an undue emphasis on the role of the professionalised 'organiser', rather than on people organising themselves. Speaking from personal experience of being on the receiving end of such 'organised' community development work, this can leave people with no greater direct say and just as disempowered as they may ordinarily be, even if the objectives are noble and social justice based (Beresford and Croft, 1988). As a result, Alinsky has come in for radical criticism for being preoccupied with leadership and shortcutting democratic involvement, rather than supporting participation. His rejection of political ideology, as if it were unnecessary baggage for any campaign, has also been rightly condemned as both untenable and ultimately self-defeating (Petcoff, 2017).

The current context of participation

A significant result of the frequent tendency to treat participation as an isolated add-on has been the failure to make broader political connections. This may have its roots in the fact that it has often been examined through the lens of public policy and services, rather than political studies, and that academia often struggles to advance interdisciplinary activity. Yet four broader stages in the development of Western representative democracy and the emergence of provisions for participation can be identified, with which it clearly makes sense to connect. The timescales offered here relate particularly to the UK and can vary with different countries. Thus:

- working for universal suffrage in representative democracy and the achievement of social rights, like the right to decent housing, education and health, from the late 19th to mid 20th century, associated with the creation of welfare states;
- provisions for participatory democracy pioneered in the area of land use planning and the expansion of community development, associated with the 1960s and 1970s;
- specific provisions for participation in health and social care policy and provision, from the 1980s through to the first decade of the 21st century;
- state reaction and service user-led renewal as conflicts and competing agendas develop, from 2010 onwards. (Beresford, 2019a)

The third stage identified approximates to UK developments like the setting up and extension of official requirements for participation in research, policy and provision. In the fourth stage, however, we can also see the increasing articulation of rifts between state/service-led ideas of participation and consumer involvement, and the pressure from citizens, service users and their allies for more say and democratic control over their lives and services and a questioning of formal arrangements, as they increasingly identified these as inadequate for their purpose (Kara, 2017; Madden and Speed, 2017; Brosnan, 2018; Rose et al, 2018; Beresford, 2018 and 2019a).

The period since 2010 has seen a strengthening of Right-wing neoliberal ideology, with an even stronger shift during the latter part of that era to populist Right-wing politics, nationally and internationally. This has developed in the US, parts of South America, Europe and the UK. While such politics are associated with demagoguery and xenophobia, these have also been linked with attacks on public services, cuts in public service budgets, and the political stereotyping and 'othering' of some groups. This tends to be at increasing odds with citizen and service user pressure for involvement and change, especially since service users – notably disabled people and mental health service users – have become particular targets. Significantly, in the UK such politics have been associated with an extreme 'welfare reform' policy which has restricted eligibility for both disability and employment benefits. The scapegoating of those receiving these benefits has been associated with little if any participation or user involvement (Stewart, 2016). Not surprisingly, dissatisfaction with promises of user involvement has become more explicit (Russo et al, 2018). Conflicts between the two competing understandings of involvement have become both more apparent and more contested, with radical new service user groupings and organisations emerging in the UK, such as Disabled People Against Cuts, Spartacus, and the Mental Health Resistance Network; these groups have been dismissive of traditional consultative involvement while in the vanguard of opposing welfare reform, especially using direct action (Beresford, 2012). This has also led to distinctions increasingly being drawn between patient and public involvement (PPI) and user-led activities and involvement, with the former treated with rising wariness, suspicion and hostility. Thus one critique dismisses formal 'public, patient involvement (PPI), as a "zombie" policy, unproductive for change and improvement' (Madden and Speed, 2017).

Co-production

Linked with this growing interest in and struggles over participation is the developing idea and practice of *co-production*. An initial categorisation adopted in relation to user involvement in research was framed in the context of knowledge production in terms of involvement, collaborative or partnership research, and user-led research. Some commentators have seen this as a continuum, from user involvement to control, others as a series of related but distinct approaches (Turner and Beresford, 2005). While there is a wariness of treating co-production as any kind of gold standard of participation, it is also seen as a more advanced approach to involvement. Its advocates highlight its potentially transformative role as a way of approaching policy, practice, learning and research which seeks to equalise power, resources, relationships, roles, risks and outcomes. It has particularly been developed in the context of professional roles and public services, where an emphasis is placed on recipients of services having their own assets, experience and abilities which can help improve policy and services (Needham and Carr, 2009). While there is no agreement about the definition of co-production, principles associated with it include:

- professionals giving up inherited power and control to work in more equal ways;
- service users and other marginalised partners having an early and equal role in agenda setting and decision-making;
- partners' experiential knowledge and lived experience being treated with equality and valued;
- giving greater consideration than usual to issues such as representation, diversity, participation and dissemination;
- supporting the empowerment of participating service users/partners to ensure they are up to speed to work in co-producing ways. This can involve a 'pre-production' stage of co-production to ensure partners are fully up to speed to work equally (Williams et al, 2020).

While some service users, their organisations and allies are advancing co-production with enthusiasm, some traditional experts are more critical of it, both diluting its meaning and highlighting what they see as weaknesses, rather than making the connections with broader inequalities and exclusions (Oliver et al, 2019). At the same time, other service user activists are calling for caution. They are sceptical about the potential of such co-production in the present unequal context of neoliberal politics and declining service provision. They see co-production currently as more an aspiration than widely achievable, stress the importance of being clear about its meaning and place more confidence in user-led initiatives for co-production than service system rhetoric or nominal requirements.

Conclusion

So, all forms of participation are complex. Participation has a long history and as has been stressed, it cannot be treated as monolithic or in isolation. Not surprisingly, it has generated much discussion and much theory. It has many ambiguities; it raises many issues and problems. This is not an argument against public participation or user involvement but against ill-informed, ambiguous, carelessly undertaken, bad and ineffective participation.

If we are serious about participation and our concern with participatory approaches to developing ideologies, then we need to address these issues, if we are to have any hope of making real participation possible.

5

Participation: challenging the barriers

A voice is a human gift; it should be cherished and used, to utter as fully human speech as possible. Powerlessness and silence go together.

Margaret Atwood, Canadian poet and writer, quoted in Adams, 2009

This chapter looks at overcoming the powerful barriers that can prevent us having any involvement in the ideologies that are the backdrop to our lives. To reiterate, the focus of this book is political ideology and the exclusion of most people from its formation and development. Ideology may be a particular example, but the reality is that most people have little involvement or say in most organisations, policies, institutions, processes and political structures that affect their lives. As we have noted, there has been an enormous increase in interest in public and other participation in recent years. Yet it remains far from a routine reality. Much of the discussion about it is simplistic and superficial – as though progressing participation is only a matter of deciding to do it. The fact that involvement is often so limited should serve as a warning that this is generally far from the case. Much more than good intentions and warm feelings are likely to be needed for it to become a reality – especially in the contentious domain of political ideology. Ironically, in recent years, some disabled people – despite being part of a marginalised group and because of their collective skill and determination – have gained more say and involvement than many non-disabled people.

For all the comforting talk about 'getting involved', 'listening to your views' and 'hearing what you say', power and wealth have arguably never been so narrowly concentrated internationally or class and global inequalities so great (Dorling, 2015). For all the rhetoric about participation and involvement, understated issues of power and power inequalities continue to be central. Power is perhaps the third crucial concept that we need to subject to more careful consideration in this discussion, since power and our relations to it are central to what say and involvement we are actually really likely to have and how far we are able to gain ownership of ideologies.

Power

In the first part of this book we encountered the two-way relationship between power and ideology. Power gives force to ideology, making it possible to impose it, while ideology is often used to legitimate power. This also leads us to issues of power and participation in relation to making change. The political sociologist Steven Lukes developed the idea of three dimensions of power. The third dimension refers to the social construction of practices, ideologies and institutions that secure people's consent to or at least acceptance of domination. Such ideological power makes it possible to influence people's wishes and thoughts, even making them want things opposed to their own self-interest, for example, convincing disadvantaged groups to support regressive public spending cuts, or older people in need of support to vote for anti-public services parties (Lukes, 2004).

The community and developmental educationalist John Gaventa drew on this to support approaches to social change rooted in the perspectives of marginalised groups and communities. Instead of looking for the sources and the solutions of social problems in the theories and ideas of social science and social policy experts, he validated the narratives of the oppressed populations involved. In Gaventa's theory, such methodological subjectivity makes it possible for the framing of a social problem and its solution, to arise from *within* the group. This both has an empowering effect on the group and provides a basis for it to take collective action to challenge dominant discourses and develop alternatives (Gaventa, 1982). Thus participation can go the whole gamut; from leaving people powerless to making them powerful, from meaning little more than being a member of a stage army, to taking the lead role in shaping debate, redefining ideas and determining action.

But there is even more to it than that. Participation may not only be variable in its purpose and effect. No less important, it is also variable in relation to *different people and groups*. This is a key issue, because it can serve both to distort the impact of participation and manipulate who gets involved and thereby what comes out of it. It is this we look at next.

Whose participation? Routine exclusions and inequalities

This was a lesson I quickly learned in the first significant work on participation in which I was involved. That was a large-scale (n: 580) survey and study of local views about a statutory participation in planning exercise in a disadvantaged inner city area and what say and involvement people felt they had locally (Beresford and Beresford, 1978; Beresford 2019b). The key findings from this study were how *little* say most people felt they had in what happened locally and in policies and services affecting them. But no less significant was the limited and biased response to the participation exercise, despite a lot of effort having been put into publicising it by the local council.

Only about one per cent of people took part in the exercise in any way and they were grossly unrepresentative of the local population, with a predominance of white middle-class participants. Groups associated with the greatest needs were least likely to take part. There was only a handful of Black people and no local youngsters present at the public meetings. Older people often felt it was time to listen to younger people, and youngsters when we knocked on doors tended to refer us to their parents, so we had to undertake a separate survey to reach them.

A particular lesson we learned was that the exercise seemed to be undermined from the start by local people's distrust of and disaffiliation from the local authority. Their hostility toward it, as we wrote at the time, meant that, 'the prevailing emotion encountered in interviewing was anger against the council, often turning into resignation in older people' (Beresford, 2019b).

Crucially, what the public participation exercise showed up was that most local people had no real sense of involvement. Nor was it just the inadequacy of existing methods of participation that seemed to account for this, but something more fundamental: people's negative feelings about the council. Their replies to our questions revealed an overwhelming sense of powerlessness. Most people felt they had little or no say in decisions affecting their area.

This offered me some key insights about participation, which my subsequent experience of citizen and user involvement has only confirmed:

- People's attitudes towards participation are strongly affected by their existing experience of authorities and power holders.

- Take up in efforts to involve people mirror broader exclusions – rather than compensate for them – unless these are determinedly challenged.
- The groups facing the greatest problems tend to correlate with those whose views are least likely to be heard.

Whatever kind or level of participation we are talking about, there is still the issue of who is likely to be able to be involved and the need to recognise that this isn't likely routinely to be equal and universal. If we are addressing participation and participatory approaches, then we need to be thinking about determinedly *inclusive* participation which seeks to address diversity with equality.

The #MeToo movement against the sexual harassment and sexual assault of women continues to tell us about routine exclusions and disempowerments, which mean that women who have been seriously abused by men are unable to speak out or have an effective voice to challenge this. What has been particularly revealing about this issue is the way that it has revealed how women who would be seen as conventionally powerful in our society have frequently shared this same experience (Hillstrom, 2019). Similarly, the Black Lives Matter movement highlights how, through successive decades and different state and federal administrations, Black men continue to be targeted by US police, with the rate of fatal shootings much higher than for other ethnic groups (Statista Research Department, 2020).

Beyond the cosy glow

While there is still a lot of lazy talk about involving people in our politics and in our world, if there's one thing this book may already be suggesting to readers, it is that such involvement is neither an easy, obvious nor commonsense affair, nor easily achieved. The lesson this author has learned from many years trying to get involved and trying to involve others on an equal basis – often at some personal cost – is that it is mostly about honesty, commitment, doing our best and trying to draw on the lessons and knowledge that others have already acquired. So I frequently find myself repeating the mantra 'half a loaf' (is better than none) .... We are unlikely to achieve as full and inclusive involvement as we want, but should never let it stop us trying and we must always be striving for it. A wide range of factors may restrict our success, but that should never be used as an excuse, stopping us reaching out and working to do better next time.

Participation, of course, is not neutral. It is itself subject to the assumptions, constraints and inequalities that operate at any time, in any society and according to the nature of any ruling ideology. Since we all of us live under such conditions and may be more or less aware of their discriminatory effects, this can mean that each of us may not only be differently positioned in relation to our opportunities to participate and exert influence, but equally, differently placed to appreciate and realise this. Paradoxically, one of the consequences of inequality can be to diminish rather than increase our awareness of power differences between us. Thus those who are granted ready access to the political and policy process can take for granted being involved, while those who are excluded may not even be aware of the extent of their marginalisation. The Left-wing writer and commentator George Orwell wrote of the way that going to one of Britain's most elite public schools, Eton College, had the effect of separating you from most other people – without you necessarily realising it. At the time of writing, the UK is yet again being led by a Prime Minister with the same isolating privilege.

The nature of exclusions

In the second half of the 20th century especially, the excluding effects of the discrimination faced by many people was highlighted and increasingly challenged through new social movements. These have notably contested racism, sexism, ageism, disablism, mentalism, and heterosexism. But the barriers to participation and pressures for unequal participation extend much further even beyond these. Thus a government-funded research and development project, by the user-led organisation and network Shaping Our Lives, has evidenced the way in which diverse involvement is restricted. It identified big barriers in the way of five major groups. Such groups of service users are excluded according to:

- equality issues: on the basis of gender, sexuality, ethnicity, class, culture, belief, age, disability, and so on;
- where they live: if they are homeless, travellers, in prison, in welfare institutions, refugees, and so on;
- communicating differently; they do not speak the prevailing language, it is not their first language, they are D/deaf and use sign language, and so on;
- the nature of their impairments: where these are seen as too complex or severe to mean they could or would want to contribute;

- where they are seen as unwanted voices: they do not necessarily say what authorities want to hear, are seen as a problem, disruptive and so on, (including neuro-diverse people and people affected by dementia). (Beresford, 2013)

This project also identified practical strategies for *overcoming* these exclusions. These all start with a commitment and determination to treat diversity with equality and inclusion as a priority. All highlight the importance of adopting a 'pro-active' approach to involvement; that is to say, putting the responsibility on yourself to make it happen rather than expecting it to come naturally to others – especially others who have faced significant oppression and discrimination. For many in that situation just surviving can be hard enough and keeping their heads down a sensible strategy for making survival possible.

What quickly became apparent from this research was that the best way of engaging with such people and groups was by reaching out to them and their communities, rather than expecting or waiting for them to come to you. Direct contact and word of mouth seem to work best. Where groups have community leaders of their own, these are an important first stop, but it is not enough just to rely on such 'community leaders'; they may be discriminatory and exclusionary in their own way too. Instead it is important to work to reach people themselves directly. Disabled people's and service users' own user-led organisations and grassroots small local community organisations are especially well placed to 'build bridges' with such 'seldom heard voices'. Disempowered groups, particularly those in residential and institutional services, are often subject to 'gatekeepers', who can stand in the way of their involvement. Sensitive and effective approaches are needed to avoid or overcome the resistance of such gatekeepers.

The disempowerment and stigma that such marginalised groups sometimes face can become internalised and then act as an additional barrier to them getting involved. To overcome such difficulties, they are likely to benefit from capacity-building to support their empowerment (see Chapter 8). Achieving effective and meaningful involvement with people whose voices are seldom heard also means exploring, evaluating and monitoring new and creative ways of engaging with and involving them – and we shall return to this shortly. The judgemental quality of public discussion about some groups, particularly around alcohol and drug use, asylum seeking and 'mental health problems', helps create and sustain negative public attitudes. Equally, groups liable to exclusion do not themselves exist in a cultural vacuum and can also exhibit negative assumptions and attitudes towards other marginalised groups. This has long provided fertile ground for divisive ideology and politics, unless combated. It is reflected at the time of writing in the kind of populist politics of former President Trump, where one marginalised group (for example, unemployed white workers in declining industries) are put at the throat of another (for example, Mexican migrants desperately seeking a life for themselves and their families).

While getting involved can mean engaging with formal arrangements for involvement, it can also mean people getting together outside of such schemes, to seek and campaign for change in more self-organised and oppositional ways. There is now increasing interest in such activity and new forms are being developed using social media and social networking sites (see Beresford and Carr, 2018). However, while involvement can be encouraged and extended by engaging with grassroots citizens' and service users' organisations, these of course themselves are not impervious to prejudice and discrimination – and this has long been traded on by demagogic politicians and their supporters. Bottom-up initiatives can be reactionary and Right-wing as well as progressive and Left-wing.

All new movements seem to have to go through a process of challenging their own discriminations and exclusions. Feminists like Audre Lorde highlighted this in relation to the women's movement (Lorde, 1984) and disabled commentators like Tom Shakespeare and Jenny Morris have done the same in relation to the disabled people's movement (Morris, 1996; Shakespeare, 2014; 2017). The Eurikha Project, supported by the Wellcome Foundation to explore the experience of people living with distress internationally, has highlighted the ways in which Black people and other ethnic groups experiencing distress have been marginalised in survivor organising in both the Global South and Global North, as well as the particular exclusions and discriminations faced by Indigenous peoples (see www.eurikha.org/about/).

Key requirements for inclusive involvement

However, it is not just that groups facing high levels of discrimination are ill-served by most arrangements for involvement. Opportunities to get involved and participatory schemes tend to leave out large swathes of the population – even where this is not necessarily the intention – and it is very unusual for participation to be anything more than a minority pursuit.

While this is so often the case and generally most people don't 'take to the streets' unless things are absolutely desperate, it does not have to be like this. But if the aim is to challenge the non-participatory nature of anything – including the development of ideology, then there must be change to make it possible.

Two components seem to be essential if people are to be able to get involved effectively and all groups are to have more equal opportunities to be involved. These are:

- Access; and
- Support.

Without *access*, all our efforts to get involved will be like banging on a closed door. Without *support*, only the best-equipped and resourced people are likely to have a say (Beresford and Croft, 1993b).

We have already touched on both these elements. Both are necessary. Experience suggests that without support, only the most confident, well-resourced, experienced and advantaged people and groups are likely to become involved. This helps explain why participatory schemes so often involve only a few people and have tended to be dominated in the West (and sometimes globally) by white middle-aged, middle-class men. Without access, efforts to become involved are likely to be difficult and ineffective, however assertive or experienced we may be. Let's look at *access* first.

Access

Access means that people have ways into organisations, agencies and institutions, groups, discussions and developments that affect them, so that they can influence, advise, inform and be part of them. This includes physical and communication access as well as other forms, like those related to culture and class. In the specific context of services and support, access also means providing services which are appropriate for and match the needs of members of different groups and communities, particularly Black and minority ethnic groups. Otherwise people will not be on the starting line for using services and getting support in which they may then want to have a say.

If people are to get involved in forums, organisations and services to influence and improve them, there need to be continuing opportunities for participation within both their organisational and political structures. This means both where control lies and where policy and practice are developed and carried out. This may include membership of governance and formal structures like committees, planning groups, and working parties, as well as involvement in substantive informal structures that exist and operate in them. Another important expression of access is for people to have control over a budget or budgets in an organisation. Cash, like knowledge, is power. It makes it possible for people to have a direct effect on what happens inside the organisation, to do things in different ways, and to achieve their own goals. The budget may be large or small. People may have control over funds for research and learning, for training and education, to develop and open up discussion, to purchase support or to undertake new projects (Beresford and Croft, 1993a and b).

Support

The need for support doesn't arise because people lack the desire or ability to participate, but because such participation is often unfamiliar and alien to them and is made difficult. There may be many obstacles in the way. People may not know what is possible or how to get involved. They may not like to ask for too much or be reluctant to complain if barriers are put in their way. The whole enterprise may seem unfamiliar, challenging and 'not for the likes' of them. There are at least five essential elements to support. These are:

- Support for personal development: to increase people's expectations, assertiveness, self-confidence and self-esteem. Assertiveness training and confidence building are crucial here.
- Support to develop skills: to build the skills that people need to participate and to develop their own ways of getting involved. A lot of speaking and writing skills are included in conventional schemes to involve people. People may want to learn more about these, but may also want to know how to challenge them and develop ways of doing things which *they* prefer and feel more familiar and at ease with.
- Practical support: to be able to get involved, including information, child care, caring support, accessible transport, meeting places, advocacy, expenses, payment for participation, and so on.
- Support for equal opportunities: provision for disabled people, D(d)eaf people, people with sensory impairments, without verbal communication, non-readers, signers, people for whom English is not their first language, and people with intellectual impairments, to get involved on equal terms.
- Support for people to get together and work in groups, including office and administrative expenses, payment for workers, training and development costs. (Beresford and Croft, 1993b, pp 52–3)

Only when these resources are present, are invitations to get involved likely to be meaningful. Anyone seeking to enable broad-based involvement, for example, as here, in the development of ideology, would do well to work hard to address them.

Disabled people: a case study

When the modern UK disabled people's movement began to form in the late 1960s and early 1970s, its pioneering members highlighted issues that seem shocking in a society that has prided itself on being a bastion of advanced Western democracy, with all the security of a modern welfare state. However, this was no shock to many disabled people. Non-disabled people began to hear of a parallel segregated world where:

- Parents having a disabled baby were encouraged to have them institutionalised or if they died, not to worry as they could 'try for a healthy one'.
- The sterilisation of disabled people was not a past horror of the Nazi regime but alive and well much later in societies like Sweden and the US that regarded themselves as civilised and egalitarian.
- Disabled people in residential homes were routinely changed into their night clothes to go to bed in the late afternoon.
- Many disabled people couldn't even get into polling stations to register their vote because these were inaccessible.
- Researchers wrote disabled people off as 'social parasites' incapable of living on their own who would always be a 'burden' on society and never be able to live on their own.

(Hunt, 1981; Coleridge, 1993; Campbell and Oliver, 1996; Oliver and Barnes, 1998; Hunt, 2019)

Segregated in 'special schools' and sometimes regarded as 'ineducable'; institutionalised in long term 'hospitals' and other institutions, still sometimes subject to physical and mental abuse there; often excluded from training, employment or promotion; impoverished; discouraged from having partner relationships and children – in some cases, as we have seen, sterilised; and often routinely denied access to the built environment and mainstream communication: these were all common experiences for disabled people.

As a result, when disabled people began to establish their movements, they almost had to start from the beginning. They were starting to do things which most others might take for granted, even if sometimes they too faced barriers and exclusions. Having been denied a voice for so long and having had others speak for them makes the disabled people's movement a particularly fruitful source of insight more generally in relation to the exclusionary nature of much discussion about ideology (Campbell and Oliver, 1996).

As one of the earliest pioneers of the UK disabled people's movement, Paul Hunt wrote in 1966: 'We are tired of being statistics, cases, wonderfully courageous examples to the world, pitiable objects to stimulate funding' (Hunt, 1966). More than 40 years later Stella Young, the late Australian comedian, was similarly challenging the traditional status imposed on disabled women like her: 'I identify very proudly as a disabled woman. I identify with the crip community. I didn't invent the word "crip". It's a political ideology I came to in my late teens and early 20s' (Young, undated). The pattern has long been set. People who are not disabled have taken it on themselves to decide what disabled people's 'problem' is, what they 'need', how to 'understand' them, make sense of their situation and its causes, what should be done about them, and what the issues are. This is essentially creating an ideology in microcosm – for and relating to a group you are not part of. But the point disabled people have made, like other groups who have been at the heart of new social movements, is that where one group decides and frames things for another, especially where there are inequalities of power and status, they tend to be discriminatory and get it wrong.

Thus the modern history of disability has been one of it largely being framed by non-disabled people as a medical and welfare problem, researched, interpreted and explained by people without direct experience of disability. The dominant way of 'understanding' disability has been of it as an isolated 'personal tragedy'. In modern times, this individualising interpretation has been overlaid with a medical model (Oliver, 1983). The solution has been seen as a two-track one; either of pressing disabled people into low grade employment or, if they are not seen as capable of this (and where the bar is drawn seems to depend more on attitudes towards disabled people and disability, rather than any objective abilities of disabled people), maintaining them on welfare benefits.

Disabled people, alongside other new social movements, offer an important case study of how people marginalised and oppressed by prevailing values and ideas can rise to the challenge of contesting this. Like all the identity-based new social movements, the disabled people's movement grew out of the sense of oppression, discrimination and exclusion felt by the people who established them. What unites welfare service user movements is that they are both based on identity and people's efforts to define their own identity through shared experience. They have all sought a revaluation of their social roles and worked to develop more positive identities.

Two groups of disabled people could be identified at the time of the founding of the disabled people's movement (and they continue to exist): those struggling to live 'in the community' and others separated off from the mainstream. Both lived restricted lives (Campbell and Oliver, 1996, p 29). An important irony in the UK was that it was some of the most marginalised and excluded disabled people who provided the vanguard that helped establish the disabled people's movement. Part of the explanation for this seems to be that, because they were seen as people who could not live their lives in mainstream society, they were segregated and lumped together in separate 'special' schools, hospitals, 'homes' and other institutions. This created unintended opportunities for these disabled people to get to know each other, develop their own shared understandings and viewpoints, and develop their own collectivity and solidarity – as disabled people. Thus institutionalisation created some of the most effective conditions for challenging it! This also highlights another overlapping distinction that can be drawn within the population of disabled people. This is between those who for one reason or another were disabled from birth or early age and those who acquired an impairment later in life, perhaps in older age. While the first group were socialised to be disabled people, we know that many of the latter group are reluctant to identify as disabled. Again, apparently paradoxically, this can weaken their possibilities of gaining a strong internalised identity as a basis for taking effective collective action (Hoban et al, 2013).

Turning ideology upside down

At a time of broader social change and ideological challenge – the 1960s onwards – disabled people's often grim and demeaning experience gave some the opportunity and impetus to question their status and situation. They both wanted what non-disabled people wanted under prevailing values and, like some non-disabled people, sometimes questioned those values. Their rising anger and frustration, the exposure of some to the new and radical politics of the time, and opportunities to explore their shared experience and develop their own ideas meant that 'a political consciousness concerning disability issues was beginning to emerge among some disabled individuals' (Campbell and Oliver, 1996, p 45), one that challenged the prevailing medicalised individualistic ideology that understood disability in terms of the individual's limitations or 'deficiencies'.

Developing participatory ideology is part of a constellation of issues that connect with politicisation and taking control. This is reflected more and less in the activities and ideas of new social movements and these, perhaps particularly the disabled people's and other service user movements, offer fundamental insights.

Big new ideas

What the emerging UK disabled people's movement did was effectively turn prevailing thinking about disability on its head. Instead of accepting non-disabled people's longstanding view of disability as a problem of broken or defective bodies, senses or minds, which meant that some disabled people were incapable of 'standing on their own two feet' and living 'independently' (that is, without external support), they developed two very different and related ideas. These reframe conventional understandings about disability. The first is the 'social model of disability', the second, the philosophy of 'independent living'. It is not possible to over-estimate the importance or indeed originality of these two ideas. They truly have been groundbreaking. They represent a radical break with traditional thinking about disability in many different ways. More than once I have heard disabled people say that being able to rethink themselves and their lives after first hearing about the 'social model', was a 'light bulb moment' for them and their lives (Morris, 1993; Thomas, 2007).

The first thing that needs to be said about these two innovative ideas is that both of them came from disabled people themselves. This represents a sea-change in developments in this field where non-disabled people have long shaped ideas and discussion. No less important, they are different in nature in almost every sense to what had gone before. Thus the social model of disability draws a distinction between impairment and disability. It defines impairment as the individual loss of or restricted function of a limb or sense. It defines disability very differently as *the negative societal response to such impairment*, whether expressed in discrimination, barriers, exclusions or negative attitudes. Thus it rejects the dominant Western view of disability as a personal misfortune or individual accident. Instead it sees disability as a particular form of social oppression, like racism, sexism or heterosexism (Oliver, 1983). Impairment is not automatically followed by disability. People with impairments need not be disabled. This is a result instead of the hostility and discrimination they experience in many societies. Since then, as debate about the social model has developed and extended, it has engaged with new issues and been the subject of much controversy and challenge. The relationship between impairment and disability, and the disabling effects of impairment have come under scrutiny (Thomas, 2007). The impact of the social model, however, has continued to be transformative, at individual political, cultural and policy levels, nationally and internationally.

The second key idea is that of 'independent living'. Historically discussion of independence in relation to disabled people has been framed in terms of their ability – or otherwise – to manage on their own, without needing additional help or support. Disabled people judged incapable of doing so (as if any of us, disabled or non-disabled, ever live entirely independently) have then been characterised as dependent. That has been the ruling definition. Disabled people's own philosophy of independence rejects this understanding and offers something very different in its place. This philosophy, building on a social model approach, identifies two key conditions for enabling disabled people to live independently. These are, first, having suitable personal support and, second, the removal of the barriers and restrictions which have prevented disabled people from living in society on equal terms with other people. Thus instead of accepting the dominant understanding of 'independence' as meaning that disabled people must be able to manage on their own, the disabled people's movement has reconceived the idea to mean providing the conditions to enable disabled people to live in society on as equal terms as possible to non-disabled people (Oliver and Barnes, 2012).

As the feminist disability commentator Jenny Morris has said, the philosophy of independent living rests on a number of key values or assumptions:

- All human life is of value.
- Anyone, whatever their impairment, is capable of exercising choice.
- People who are disabled by society's reaction to physical, intellectual and sensory impairment and to emotional distress have the right to assert control over their lives.
- Disabled people have the right to participate fully in society.

(Morris, 1993, p 21)

Independent living is enshrined in the UN Convention on the Rights of Persons with Disabilities. This is having a growing impact on politics and policies relating to disabled people, not least in the Global South.

How disabled people highlighted participation

How did they do this? This group – disabled people – facing some of the most severe discriminations and exclusions in society. How did they find a way radically to rewrite prevailing understandings of themselves and create fundamentally different ones? How have they managed to make such a challenge to prevailing disability ideology, when we know from the journey we have already made in this publication, how difficult it can be to formulate and take control of ideologies, rather than merely being on the receiving end of those of other powerful interests? The disabled people's movement offers some unique clues because of the particular barriers facing disabled people.

Often, their exclusion is not even seen as an issue. So, for example, Rosa Parks's refusal in Montgomery, Alabama in 1955 to give up her seat in a 'colored section' of a bus to a white passenger after the whites-only section was filled made worldwide news and heralded major social change; years later, wheelchair users were still having to chain themselves to buses to highlight the way they were routinely debarred from so-called 'public transport' in London and elsewhere.

How disabled people have countered these barriers offers important insights into how we can take control of ideologies more generally and develop our own. Together with insights from other new social movements, it offers in microcosm understanding of both the problems and ways of overcoming them.

PART III

Towards participatory ideology

6

Learning to work together: the key to inclusive involvement

> I think Americans generally are not used to working very hard,
> in terms of working for the collective. I think in our country
> we have taken individualism to its farthest reaches, possibly.
> Alice Walker, writer and activist, undated

A core theme running through this book is the need to connect two key concepts and discourses: ideology and participation. In this third part of the book, we focus on one of the most effective ways of doing this – through working together to take collective action.

This is because we have already discovered that there is a third concept central to this relationship between participation and ideology: power – and inequalities of power. Participation at its most meaningful is about recognising the significance of power and challenging such inequalities of power. At the heart of this is finding ways of maximising our own power when we seek to influence existing structures and exercise an effective say of our own. As we have seen, mostly in Western societies, we are used to and encouraged to try and do this on our own. Thus the *individualised* complaints procedures and consumerist market research and opinion-seeking routes we are offered under the dominant exchange relationships of the market. Such individualised approaches to rectification have been advanced as more collective approaches to consumer protection – through legislation, free legal aid and representation – have been reduced and undermined.

Such individualised responses are an essential limitation of such approaches; it is usually only where more collective models are employed, ranging from class actions to statutory provisions for consumer rights, that effective challenge becomes possible. We are flattered into believing the exchange relationships of consumerism put us into the position of kings and queens, but of course generally acting on our own, we have no kingdom to defend us. While academic talk of welfare state relationships, putting us in the position of passive pawns, flattered new Right political masters who were privatising public services in the 1990s, it cynically ignored the safeguards that state welfare had offered for the health and wellbeing of the nation (Le Grand, 1997).

Central to challenging unequal and excluding relations, systems and indeed political ideologies is working together for change. All effective struggles are collective struggles. It's written into our culture, thus sayings like 'Strength through numbers', 'Workers united will never be defeated' and so on. But it would be a mistake to assume that this realisation and reality only applies to the oppressed and 'masses'. It's for the same reasons that power holders seek to work together, sometimes illegally through combines, monopolies and betting rings. Working together, rather than fighting or competing, works well for rich and poor, powerful and powerless alike. We should remember that. It is key to gaining a say and it is central to any shift to the participatory development of ideology.

The disabled people's movement is an outstanding example of a group or constituency learning to work together to challenge exclusion and disempowerment. For this reason it is worth staying with them as a case study for developing our exploration of advancing participatory ideology. They are not only a significant example of this, they have had to do so in the face of many more barriers or exclusions than many groups face. They have generated and developed vital new concepts for working together in the process, such as self-advocacy, accessibility, self-organisation, experiential knowledge and emancipatory research.

Learning from the disabled people's movement

Years after its foundation, Stella Young, the Australian disabled comedian we have already heard from, summed up the strength of feeling and the social insight that gave strength to the disabled people's movement from the start: 'I am not your inspiration, thank you very much. My disability exists not because I use a wheelchair, but because the broader environment isn't accessible' (Young, undated). So how is it that the international disabled people's movement has been able collectively to advance so much in developing its own progressive and participatory ideology and ideas and managed successfully to challenge existing dominant ones? How has a group often stereotyped as dependent and defective achieved far more than so many others? We will find ourselves encountering some unexpected contradictions as we try and find the answer to these questions. But they are likely to help lead us in useful directions for charting the way to less externally shaped and controlling political ideology.

Pressures for participation

First, perhaps we should again remind ourselves of the levels of oppression that disabled people have experienced over the years, both in the (post-)industrial Western world and the Global South. This may help us to appreciate how it is the movement has achieved what it has. The oppression disabled people have faced is beyond the conventional marginalisation and exclusion associated with poverty, disenfranchisement and being devalued. As we have seen, disabled people have been subjected to the most severe curtailments of liberty, including: euthanasia, extermination and sterilisation; the denial of parenthood, movement, employment and family life; routine institutionalisation and segregation; invasive surgery in childhood; and removal from their parents. Mental health service users have long been subjected to compulsory 'treatment' and constraint, whose effects can include long-term health damage and premature death as well as the routine undermining of their consciousness, feelings and emotions. Paradoxically, we can see how such appalling oppression has actually worked to advance disabled people's efforts to liberate themselves – creating a spur for self-generated change (Coleridge, 1993; LeFrancois et al, 2013).

In my view there are at least four factors at work which help explain the successful emergence of the disabled people's movement. These are:

1. the *extent* of oppression and marginalisation facing disabled people;
2. their enforced collectivity and other unintended opportunities available as a result for them to challenge their oppression;
3. the movement's coincidence with broader political, policy, technical, cultural and social changes;
4. disabled people's need to do things differently because of the very nature of their impairments and disability.

First, as we have already seen, disabled people globally have frequently faced the most extreme levels of oppression and discrimination, usually only associated with the punishment of criminals or treatment of enemies in wartime. These can extend to every aspect of their life, imposing restrictions and constraints. Opportunities for such treatment are magnified because of the reliance of some disabled people on assistance for the daily tasks of life like dressing, going to the toilet, washing and other bodily functions. But it can also be because of stereotypes of their incapacity and dependence – as if they are incapable of independent thought or action and treated as if lacking any autonomy. The resulting restrictions on rights and liberty, often accompanied by institutionalisation, have provided an especially fierce impetus for many disabled people to struggle for change in their conditions. The heavily stigmatised status of disabled people has also discouraged non-disabled people from taking on the role. Thus the old charity advertisement showing a disabled person's parking space with the caption, 'Is this the only time you put yourself in our place?' However, it has not stopped non-disabled people from speaking on disabled people's behalf, with traditional charities 'for' disabled people, led and shaped *by* non-disabled people (Campbell and Oliver, 1996; Oliver and Barnes, 2012).

Second, however, one of the ironies relating to the experience of disabled people is that discriminatory policies intended to segregate them from non-disabled people and lump them together as dependent, have actually had some unintended *positive* effects. They have provided opportunities for disabled people to challenge dominant views about them, to build solidarity and develop collective action. This has been true of both the development of segregated 'special' schools and colleges for disabled people and the institutionalisation of younger disabled people in residential homes. Thus the UK disabled people's movement has significant origins among disabled people segregated and congregated in the residential services of the Leonard Cheshire Foundation. Colleges for young disabled people, like Treloars and Hereward College in England, have not only sought to harness and develop their skills and ambitions, but have also incidentally offered the conditions for them to develop their confidence, solidarity and collectivity. While this is hardly an argument for such segregated education, its decline has also meant the loss of reinforcement for a positive disabled identity and of a traditional source for the development of mutuality and collectivity among disabled people. What we can say, though, is that counter-intuitively, the emergence of the UK disabled people's movement seems to have been assisted by these two earlier and ostensibly counter-developments (Campbell and Oliver, 1996; Hunt, 2019).

Third, the emergence of service user movements, with their commitment to people speaking and acting for themselves, also greatly benefited from the more general development of new social movements. The leaders of the disabled people's and service user movements were quick to articulate their indebtedness to these movements and were happy to learn from the experience of the feminist, Black civil rights and LGBTQ movements, recognising the overlaps and the importance of intersectionality. This was just one of the social changes that worked to the advantage of welfare service user movements. We should also remember that disabled people may also be women, Black and gay, so there are important overlaps encouraging cross-fertilisation between movements (Shakespeare et al, 1997; Thomas, 2007).

Another development that also opened doors initially, again surprisingly and contradictorily, was the international shift to the political and ideological Right during the 1970s. The new political Right's preoccupation with the market and market consumerism, with its dislike of state intervention, played to some of the concerns and ambitions of service users, even if in the longer term it has curtailed the formal support available to them. It gave added weight to their desire to have greater rights and say at the receiving end of public services and, for some time at least, the conflicting objectives of managerialist consumerism and liberatory self-advocacy seemed to reflect common concerns for more say and involvement. This provided early opportunities for the disabled people's and other service user movements to achieve progressive policy changes. However, much of this progress has been lost as neoliberal pressure for austerity and 'welfare' and public spending cuts has increased.

Fourth and finally, disabled people have had to develop different innovative ways to get involved individually and collectively because, by the very nature of their impairments and the discriminatory and excluding responses these often result in, many are unable to get involved in the conventional ways. Thus in a world where the built environment often excludes disabled people and where prevailing methods of communication may be inaccessible to them, disabled people have had to develop new accessible ways to be involved. It is important to remember, for example, that even the accessibility for disabled people of formal arrangements for voting at elections has not been recognised as an issue until recently, and that some mental health service users and people with learning difficulties have actually been denied the right to vote. Such exclusions have also meant that disabled people have placed an emphasis on their own self-empowerment as a basis for effective collective action, while also recognising that developing their own collectivity is one of the most helpful preconditions for inclusive collective action (Oliver and Barnes, 2012; Beresford, 2013; Beresford and Carr, 2018).

The urgency to innovate

The barriers we have identified here highlight issues of physical and communication access. Disabled people have determinedly addressed these in order to work together in different ways and to communicate in more accessible and inclusive ways, including the use of 'easy to read' materials and information provided in non-written and non-verbal ways. Their innovation has included the development of new approaches to and forms of 'direct action' that people can take part in regardless of some impairments. They have also maximised the use of new technology both in order to work collectively and also to engage in the social sphere even though they may be restricted to their home or have very limited energy. There have been many barriers to the active involvement of disabled people and addressing those that affect one group does not necessarily enable the inclusion of another nor make it possible for people with different impairments or issues to do things together. Disabled people and their organisations have made enormous progress in overcoming these barriers as well as in highlighting more broadly the need to do so.

Thus to summarise, we have seen disabled people internationally at the vanguard of developing their own collective ideology and action. They have made this possible by adopting very effective strategies and tactics. These include:

- Their willingness and skill in learning from the experience of other movements and campaigns.
- Their recognition of the value of a separatist approach to achieving ultimate inclusion in mainstream society; working together in their own discrete organisations, while engaging with existing systems with great skill.
- They have recognised the importance of developing their own research, knowledges, philosophy, ideas and theories.
- They have developed the idea of empowerment as a basis for both personal development and collective action.
- They have sought to address the desire for more inclusivity in their own ranks, both highlighting inequalities, for example, in relation to diversity, and seeking to overcome these.

While highlighting these achievements, we should not forget the reaction they have encountered, because there certainly has been one. This has come from Right-wing politics and ideology and through the welfare system it has been restructuring in its own image. Policymakers have sought to subvert the reforms that the disabled people's movement have worked for and ideologues have attacked them with so-called 'welfare reform', which has undermined their human and civil rights, impoverished them and increased their insecurity (Stewart, 2016;

Barnett-Cormack, 2018). This is a reminder of the constant pressures against participation both in ideology and beyond. It is also a reminder of the central importance of being able to work effectively *collectively* to challenge this and pursue the social and political change to which you are committed.

Developing our own collectivity

The efforts of disabled people offer enormous insights for non-disabled people seeking to work collectively in inclusive ways. They can not only help those who are not disabled to involve disabled people, but also support all of us in our efforts to involve everybody in as inclusive and equal ways as possible. The first step to making this change is in one sense a small one. It's been well summed up by people as different as Gloria Steinem, the US feminist and activist, and Boots Riley, the rapper and film director:

> Every social justice movement that I know of has come out of people sitting in small groups, telling their life stories, and discovering that other people have shared similar experiences. (Shriver, 2011)

> Any collective action is made up of individuals who one day decided not to sit and watch anymore. (Riley, undated)

The point is, we *can* make a difference – together – and it can be just a small step beyond teaming up with a few like-minded people. But a lot of us don't get to that point, we don't take that first step recommended by Boots Riley and Gloria Steinem. By contrast, many of us have been taught and have internalised a version of history and change which seems to be based on the 'great (white) man' (rarely woman) theory of events and progress. No matter if this bears little relation to historical reality.

Of course, individuals can and do make a difference. What would the effects on England and France have been if Joan of Arc had not been burnt at the stake? What difference would it have made for African Americans if the assassination attempts on Malcolm X, Fred Hampton or Martin Luther King had failed? Say there had been no Winston Churchill waiting in the wings in 1940? What direction would a Labour government have taken in 1997 if its Labour leader John Smith hadn't died prematurely? And so on, and so on. These historical might-have-beens are fascinating – if ultimately futile to consider.

Challenging individualising assumptions

But even if we have been taught the 'great leader' version of history –
from Alexander the Great, through Julius Caesar, to Catherine the
Great and Napoleon, with the rest of us generally, and often actually,
cast in the role of stage army – when it comes to bringing about
change, whether in ideology or regime, it's difficult even to pretend that
individual action is likely to make much difference. Instead opposition,
challenge and resistance are more likely to be associated with people
getting together, working together, *organising*. That way, they are much
more likely to have some hope of success.

However, in individualising societies like the UK and US, we are still
encouraged to believe that we're better off trying to do things on our
own, rather than joining forces with others. While there are elements
of joint work at school, not to forget team sports (which are often more
about competitiveness and winning rather than working together),
we quickly learn that we will largely be judged on our own, through
individual exam results, assessed work or individual annual reviews. Thus
the inherent contradiction of the idea of 'meritocracy': that individuals
can be rewarded according to their individual achievement, when that
is only really achievable through making broader social change together.
And, while much sport is played in teams, these are organised almost
as much to be competitive within, as against opponents, with people
having to fight for their place, justify their selection, be seen to be 'good',
be judged by their peers. It's ironic that so much of school seems to be
about competing rather than collaborating with each other, although
it is meant to be about our socialisation as citizens. No wonder there is
so much bullying still in schools and many of us do not look back on
those times as anything like 'the best days of our life'!

Consumerist thinking, as we have seen, also encourages us to believe
that the 'customer is king' and that we can win on our own. TV
consumer rights programmes show people who have previously been
badly treated by companies win out and seem to vindicate this view.
What we are really seeing, of course, is the power of big TV companies
and high audience programmes – and the corresponding reluctance of
suppliers of goods and services to be shown as nasty and unbending to
audiences of millions. In reality, the individual can be easily ignored
or picked off and more often is. The truth is that there is 'strength in
numbers' and it's less 'too many cooks spoiling the broth' than 'many
hands make light work'.

Of course, people actually do lots of things together. There is nothing
very remarkable about getting together in groups to do things. This

happens routinely with reading groups, hobby, social and activity clubs. These can be informal or adopt traditional formal democratic structures, with committees, chairs and set procedures. Two academics helpfully coined the term 'organising around enthusiasms' to describe such freely given activity, which involves work but remains leisure rather than employment and where people might indulge their passions collectively by participating in groups (Hoggett and Bishop, 1986). So getting together to do things can be unremarkable for many of us. It is something we choose to do, enjoy doing, do for the love of it, rather than for any monetary reward or because we have to.

But, and it is another big but, this same tradition does not seem to apply when it comes to politics and ideology. Perhaps this is because issues of power, inequalities of power and individual ambitiousness are so central to and come so close to the surface in these domains (even when they are ostensibly about challenging them). These also generally tend to be minority activities, with tendencies to conflict and divisiveness as we saw in Chapter 3. In countries like the UK, even when membership of mainstream political parties is high (as with the Labour Party under Jeremy Corbyn), it generally only reflects a small minority of the population. Many more people are likely to vote in TV talent contests than they are for local mayors or in local referenda. Even fewer of us are active members of trades unions or active in political parties. It is perhaps not surprising when we consider more closely what such 'involvement' and 'activism' may actually mean. It tends to entail a whole round of dreary activities: cold calling on the phone, knocking on doors, stuffing envelopes, leafleting and fundraising. It can bring an endless cycle of long meetings, heavy on procedures, not necessarily the sort of thing we want to do in our ever-declining much-valued 'spare time'. It can all feel far removed from the power and policymaking of politicians in parliaments, and often has little power to influence these.

Some problems of conventional collectivity

Counterpoised against this has been the idea of the 'tyranny of structurelessness', proposed in the 1970s by the feminist Jo Freeman, in relation to more recent, would-be liberatory ways of working together. Freeman argued that, while the aims and rhetoric might be of equality, inclusion and participation, the actual and substantive ways in which power relations might work in collective situations could also be very unequal. An apparent lack of structure could actually often disguise an informal, unrecognised and unaccountable leadership that was all the more insidious because its very existence was denied (Freeman, 1972–3). Thus some would be seen and treated as more important than others, counting effectively as particularly powerful or influential 'heavy votes' – which in Orwell's words would be 'more equal' than others (Orwell, 1945).

Meanwhile, being involved in more radical organisations may demand more active engagement and more hands-on activities than joining major parties. This may extend to attending public meetings, demonstrating, picketing, planning photo opportunities and organising events, but whether it actually offers any more real say and control, may be debatable. And how much it constitutes truly collective action, rather than being a 'stage army' or 'making up the numbers', is also often open to question. Furthermore, bigger questions are beginning to be raised about how effective such traditional expressions of protest and challenge are (Heller, 2017).

All these potentially unequal ways of working are not only unlikely to be inclusive and effective. They can also be rather unpleasant, dreary and devalued. They can be alienating, distressing and nasty. No wonder then, that so many people are put off such political involvement because the human costs can seem so high. And this at a time when people are having to work longer and longer hours in globalised neoliberal economies and there is less and less state support for many as parents, grandparents and caring for others. People who get involved in order to make change begin to learn instead the sad lesson that the subtext of such activity is often to realise the complex personal or political agendas of others and their organisations and how these advance others' individual ambitions and/or political careers.

However, this is not a necessary or inevitable lesson to be learned. Rather perhaps the key learning is that if we do want to be part of progressive change, then we must put much more emphasis into *how* we seek to achieve it and the kind of approaches to participating we will work for and adopt. The old pseudo-democratic ways need to be reviewed; the newer ostensibly more 'touchy feely' ones need to be subjected to more rigorous critique. Most of all we need to build our own organisations that are rooted in a commitment to working inclusively, equally and participatorily, building on the knowledge and experience that already exists. In the next chapter, we will start looking at how we may best be able to do this.

7

Developing our own organisations

> The greatest humanistic and historical task of the oppressed: to liberate themselves.
>
> Paulo Freire, Brazilian educator and philosopher, 1972, p 3

Once we start thinking about the value of getting organised and working together – in this case to have an effective voice in developing and shaping political ideology, then we need to think about developing our own groups, our own organisations, that is to say self-organisations, run by the people they are for, rather than set up by others for them. Such organisations are the physical expression of most movements. Nowadays, they can take many forms, from virtual groupings that connect people through social networking, through to the most traditionally structured bodies that are nonetheless still based on the principle of self-organising – getting together to make change on your own behalf (Beresford and Carr, 2018, pp 289–335).

It is important to make clear, as we seek to operationalise the argument for participatory ideology, that not all organising and collective working is based on the principle of self-organising. Guy Standing, the economist and professor of development studies, has expressed the conventional view that collective action per se is enough, when he argues: 'Collective action remains the best way of renewing the march towards the great trinity of liberty, equality, and solidarity' (Standing, 2015). Huey Newton, however, the African-American activist and co-founder of the Black Panther Party, offered a word of warning, reminding us that even reform and radical organisations can lose sight of what they are meant to be doing or fail to offer what's needed:

> You can tell the tree by the fruit it bears. You see it through what the organization is delivering as far as a concrete program. If the tree's fruit sours or grows brackish, then the time has come to chop it down – bury it and walk over it and plant new seeds. (Findley, 1972)

The centrality of shared experience

This has led me to the view that the best basis for organising and working together is likely to be shared experience. I have come to that conclusion from my own direct involvement in collective action and indeed that of countless others. Having something in common that unites us and means we have a shared experience – of discrimination or oppression – seems to be a powerful enabler of effective collective working. It highlights our commonalities and does not deny our differences. Many of the new social movements that have come to be understood in terms of 'identity politics' may perhaps be more helpfully understood as movements based on shared lived experience. What unites us is this related experience, not a uniform identity. It is for this and other reasons that the notion of identity politics has been challenged, ideas of intersectionality applied to it and the importance of diversity highlighted (Lloyd, 2005; Yuval-Davis, 2006).

A further issue now enters the picture. This makes it even more complicated and, indeed, seems both contradictory and unhelpful. When people work for change, it is often, even if not always, because they want to be treated as equals – the same as other people – to be part of the mainstream, alongside others, rather than seen as different, inferior, 'other' and lumped together with other people seen in the same negative way and segregated from the rest. But if the aim is inclusion, then what we seem to be saying here is that the route to it is to separate yourself off in your own groupings, tied to your different experience.

Indeed we are saying this, as countless activists and movements before us have done. Because what we are talking about here is recognising and highlighting experience that is devalued and discriminated against, in order to challenge that exclusion and discrimination. And the only way we can do that effectively is to start from the position of that experience and place an emphasis on it. We'll come onto the complexities of such experience later on, but meanwhile we need to consider this issue more carefully. You can make more sense of it, if you start by considering what tends to happen if such first-hand experience is not the demarcator of such collective organising. We should also stress again here that, while much of the discussion that has been associated with the emergence of 'new social movements' has been framed in terms of identity, with them cast as identity-based movements, here our stress is on *experience*; direct, lived, similar, shared and common experience, as a basis for unity, collectivity and working together. Clearly there are overlaps between identity and experience but they are *not* the same.

First, we have to say that having such shared lived experience frequently is *not* the basis for collective action. There is an obvious reason for this. Groups getting together to make change are frequently disempowered and marginalised groups, facing oppression. That's why they get together – it is a sharp spur to try to change that! But by definition if they are less powerful, then they are likely to be overshadowed by more powerful people and groups. Such groups may not only be the ones who are overpowering them. These may also be people and groups who are happy to speak on their behalf, reducing the strength of their own voice in the process. Thus the contradiction that while historically as a group, men have oppressed women; white people oppressed Black people and heterosexuals done the same to gays, lesbians, bi-sexual, transgender and Queer people, they have also from their position of power often spoken for them, imposing their own interpretations and prescriptions. At a societal level this may be described as hetero-patriarchalism; at a personal level, as 'mansplaining'. In this author's view it is inherently disempowering and oppressive.

From personal experience, this phenomenon of marginalised groups being drowned out in collective action is common in community organising, where much campaigning takes place. Here inequalities of power tend to mean that 'leaders' are more likely to have the political status and cultural equipment (and even time and opportunity) to engage, than those who may be the most disadvantaged by the problems under consideration. This has also been reinforced by the professionalisation of such activity (Beresford and Croft, 1988; Petcoff, 2017). Historically such campaigning has tended to reflect the exclusions and discriminations of the wider society, thus to be led by white middle-class professionals rather than the poor, working-class people who are most at the mercy of the social problems such campaigns are ostensibly concerned with. It can be difficult to challenge this, since those advantaged activists can reasonably claim that, as 'local people' themselves, they have a right to speak and perhaps even that without them doing so, less valued voices will just be ignored.

I witnessed an illuminating example of this when undertaking a research project in a traditional urban city area that was undergoing a process of gentrification. The traditional working-class population had very different aspirations for their area and understandings of 'community' than the middle-class incomers. But when it came to setting up a community centre and association, it was the latter who dominated and it was their proposals that triumphed. Thus although we found that locals wanted a bar in the community building, incomers did not, but instead more 'cultural' activities. It was the latter that went ahead (Beresford and Croft, 1986).

There is nothing like shared experience, especially difficult experience, for creating common bonds and common goals. To meet others who have been through the same as us, who have faced the same difficulties and the same struggles, can have effects beyond our wildest expectations. It really can change our lives. I'll say more about this when I return to the idea of empowerment shortly. Having shared experience takes us beyond the intellectual, beyond our ordinary politics, because it gets to the heart of us; beyond how we have learnt to present ourselves, how we are expected to think and behave according to dominant values and expectations, to how and who we truly are – to our versions of ourselves and the world we live in. That is why it has such power as a mobiliser of collective action and common commitment.

Of course, we must also remember that people's experience tends to be multifaceted. As the theory of intersectionality reminds us, we may have many intersecting experiences and identities. The concept of community is one that is as much based on exclusion as inclusion. We may be valued as a professional but devalued as Black and/or LGBTQ. The complexity of identity and the limitations of 'identity politics' are well rehearsed (Coaston, 2019). Later we will return to the issues raised by taking as our starting points our lived experience and 'experiential knowledge'.

We may be valued because of wider recognition of our shared oppression, while at the same devalued because of our difference; because of our age, gender, ethnicity, sexuality culture, belief, class or so on. The emergence of new social movements, which we touched on in Chapter 6, from the 1960s onwards – first the Black people's and women's movement, then the LGBTQ and older people's movement (for example, the Grey Panthers) – can be seen as direct expressions of this. Groups involved were highlighting that they were doubly marginalised; first by dominant politics and ideology, and then by counter politics and ideology (Lent, 2002). Women were making clear that engaging in struggles over inferior pay and work conditions, child care or violence against them, tended not to be given priority in mainstream campaigns and collective action (Lister, 1991). In such organising, historically, some have been more equal than others. It was not that it was impossible to make some progress in such broader organisations and campaigns but, like the first wave feminists who organised as suffragettes in the early 20th century, such doubly marginalised groups were more likely to make progress on their own (Rowbotham, 1973; 1989).

This meant establishing their own organisations, based on their own values and ideas – their own ideologies, rather than being subordinated in those of other people/men. Of course every group facing exclusion also includes people subject to further discrimination, for example, on the basis of protected characteristics. The campaign for recognition as one marginalised group is almost invariably followed by more campaigns from within that group for recognition of other exclusions faced by its members. These are often trivialised in terms of 'political correctness' and now also 'wokeness', but in a world of discrimination it is no joke to be a Black disabled lesbian parent and to be treated as if at the bottom of a pile, subject to oppression relating to every aspect of your identity and experience.

As we have seen, this was recognised in the 1980s by the feminist Left and gave birth to the Beyond The Fragments movement which sought to work in more inclusive and equal ways (Rowbotham et al, 1979). Sadly, we may judge from the continuing divisions that operate on the political Left (and indeed on the political Right) that its hopes were not fulfilled, even if it developed experience and highlighted ways of working that might be more fruitful.

At the same time, it has also been argued that the emergence of identity politics has weakened and undermined the possibilities for solidarity associated with earlier class-based struggles. There can undoubtedly be tensions between diversity and solidarity. The unfamiliar often seems to be interpreted by human beings as threatening and dangerous. This is a fear that ideologues have long played upon, building hate between groups on the basis of ignorance and difference. However, by contrast, what we have found in Shaping Our Lives, the user-led organisation, is that efforts to be inclusive have actually strengthened solidarity by helping people get a better understanding of the experiences of others and the benefits of including and working with them (Beresford and Branfield, 2012).

Pride (https://en.wikipedia.org/wiki/Pride(2014_film)), the 2014 British film, offers a powerful and highly visible example of the complexity of issues of diversity, solidarity and inclusion. Set at the time of the contentious UK coalminers' strike of 1984–5, a group of lesbians and gay men (Lesbians and Gays Support the Miners – LGSM) make a decision to raise funds for the impoverished striking miners. However, some of the miners and their families are initially reluctant to be associated with LGSM or to take their money. The film shows how, although the strike failed, there were big successes in developing understanding and solidarity between different movements and campaigning groups. Significantly and again highlighting the complex relationship between solidarity and treating diversity with equality, in November 1984, a group of lesbians broke away from LGSM to form a separate group, Lesbians Against Pit Closures, although some lesbians remained active in the LGSM campaign rather than joining the women-only group.

Organising and disabled people

Now we want to focus further on disability, disabled people and the self-organising of disabled people: we believe it has powerful and particular insights to offer in the present context. This is because critical to the effectiveness of the disabled people's movement has been its development of its own organisations and its own ways of taking collective action.

Disability organising and campaigning have long been owned by non-disabled people. Disabled people themselves were at best marginal to the resulting organisations internationally. It was the emergent disabled people's movement that first identified this as a problem and struggled to find new ways of 'self organising'. While there were precedents for such disabled people-led collectivism over several centuries, the international disabled people's movement that emerged in the last quarter of the 20th century represented a much more radical departure.

It has drawn a distinction between:

- **Organisations *for* disabled people** – which are controlled by non-disabled people. In the UK, these have been associated with big charities like the Leonard Cheshire Foundation, Mencap and Scope (formerly the Spastics Society), which have traditionally campaigned on the basis of a single condition, appealing to the pity and 'generosity' of donors and frequently presenting disabled people in paternalistic, demeaning and 'othering' terms through their media representation. More recently such organisations have placed an increasing emphasis on their own organisational brand and imperatives and celebrity endorsement in fund-raising rather than the provision of services and support.

And those:

- **Organisations *of* disabled people** – which disabled people establish and control themselves. These have been committed to a rights-based rather than welfare 'needs' approach to challenging disability, emphasising equality, anti-discrimination, inclusion and social justice, developing new forms of support and new approaches to inclusion.

While the value base of traditional disability organisations was often confused and unclear, the new disabled people's organisations in the UK were firmly rooted in the social model (of disability) and the philosophy of independent living. However, it is not just that disabled people's own organisations contested traditional analyses and responses to disability and sought to develop their own. They have also tried to work in fundamentally *different* ways. This is not surprising given that their origins were very different to traditional disability organisations (Oliver, 1983; Oliver and Barnes, 1998).

The disabled people who set up their own organisations did so not from a professional, policy, charitable or ideological purpose, but because of their own lives and experience and their primary desire to improve these and those of other disabled people. Such disabled people-led organisations, as Jane Campbell and Mike Oliver, founding members of the UK disabled people's movement, have written,

> provided both emotional and practical support which was of immense value to many disabled people. The emotional dimensions is captured by Elsa Becket: 'The fact was that there were disabled people together unashamedly and unselfconsciously talking about disability, talking about their experience.' (Quoted in Campbell and Oliver, 1996, pp 51–2)

Some disabled people who got involved were also able to engage with existing political ideologies from their own enthusiasms and bring those to bear on the disability issues they now sought to make new sense of. Like other new social movements, the disabled people's movement was not immune to the problems arising from existing social divisions. Later we will see how they sought to address these. Meanwhile, these disabled people's organisations tended to feel very different to conventional charitable and other 'organisations *for*'. I can certainly report this from my own experience, particularly in relation to the early days of the psychiatric system survivor movement.

> When I went to my first meeting of Survivors Speak Out (one such national 'user led organization') in 1987, it just felt different to anything else. Looking back that is mainly because of how it allowed me to think about myself. It was a big meeting with lots of people there,

allies as well as survivors and on the surface – given it was held in a conventional community space with rows of chairs and speakers at the front, you could say it was pretty conventional. But that's only the surface. People would be going in and out all the time, so they could take time out as they needed. There was lots of chatter. But most of all and rapidly dawning on me as a recently hospitalized mental health service user, still not feeling too brilliant, it was just the atmosphere of openness that defined and distinguished it. People were saying things you wouldn't usually expect people to say. They were talking openly about their situation, their difficulties. They were friendly. For the first time since all this had happened to me I had the sense I could *be myself*. You may not know how unusual this can feel to someone experiencing distress. I could be truthful. I didn't have to check out anything I said. There would be other people who would understand routinely. I could meet kindred spirits, who wouldn't question, who wouldn't look strangely and what's more this was also an organization that was about doing something to change things for the better – from that starting point. For me it was a new departure. We are talking about a sense of understanding, of acceptance, of valuing, of equality and openness. (Beresford, 2010, p 91)

Ken Davis, a pioneer of the UK disabled people's movement, described the Union of the Physically Impaired Against Segregation (UPIAS), an early and highly effective UK disabled people's organisation, as 'the intellectual and political heart of the movement', but also stressed that 'behind that there were the most enormous personal, intensely supportive relationships going on all the way down the line, with members nearly killing themselves to support each other to be active in the debates' (Campbell and Oliver, 1996, p 68).

The very different ways in which traditional disability organisations and the new disabled people's organisations work was highlighted by a key initiative of UPIAS, the publication in 1976 of its Fundamental Principles of Disability (UPIAS/Disability Alliance, 1976). This was a detailed account of a discussion between UPIAS and a more traditional non–user-led disability organisation about ways forward for disabled people. It highlights the large and growing gulf between both the ways of working and approaches of these contrasting organisations. One, the Disability Alliance, highlights the role of 'professional expertise' and analysis, the conventional political process and a top-down approach to change, based on Fabian ideology, seeking to influence 'public opinion'. The other, UPIAS, emphasises democratic process and accountability, a bottom-up and extra-parliamentary approach rooted in the disabled people's movement and a participatory and emancipatory ideology (UPIAS/Disability Alliance, 1976).

The dialogue between the two organisations highlights the enormous distance between traditional Fabian approaches to social policy and new participatory ones, where groups on the receiving end of social policy challenge the right of others to speak for them, developing their own collectivities, ideas and theories, rejecting traditional 'expertise' and emphasising the expertise that came from direct or lived experience. One commentator exploring new social movements concluded that the discussion, 'was supposedly designed to see whether UPIAS could join the Alliance and whether Alliance members would be allowed to affiliate to UPIAS. In effect, however, it simply emphasised the irreconcilability of the old moderate approach and the new, self-organised radicalism' (Lent, 2002, pp 107–8). There are also power inequalities that need to be recognised – for example, between the famous sociologist leader of the Disability Alliance (Peter Townsend) and the unresourced disabled people who met with him. But equally, despite the liberatory and egalitarian ideals of UPIAS, other inequalities also need to be acknowledged, as reported in Jane Campbell's and Mike Oliver's history of the UK disabled people's movement – for instance, views from two disabled women, who became significant in the movement:

'I had already met the UPIAS when I was at school. Briefly [they] had been down to [the school] one weekend and they'd done a presentation and it went down like a cup of cold sick, quite honestly.'

'I was pleased to know [that UPIAS existed], but having been emotionally and intellectually battered to the floor by one of its leaders, it did not feel it was like anything to which I wanted to belong.' (Quoted in Campbell and Oliver, 1996, p 52)

Clearly it would be a mistake to offer any organisation, any movement, in simplistic terms as transcending the many exclusions and inequalities that can operate in societies. This was no more true of the disabled people's than of other movements. However, while accepting that human reach may often exceed its grasp, some key gains and differences do emerge, and can be seen with self-organising and self-defining approaches to collective action, which have an important bearing on moving to more participatory approaches to the development of political ideology. We will now look in more detail at these, building on the particular experience of the disabled people's movement and its user-led organisations.

Doing things differently: a case study

I am offering as an example, Shaping Our Lives, which defines itself as a 'user-led organisation' and in which I have long been actively involved. Shaping Our Lives has been in existence for more than twenty years. It's main aims are to increase the say and control that disabled people and other long-term users of health and social care (for example, mental health service users/survivors, older people, people with learning difficulties, and those with long-term and/or life-limiting conditions) have over their lives and over policies and services that affect them. It is also strongly committed to addressing diversity in relation to conventional equality issues. In this it could be argued it is not necessarily any different from traditional disability organisations. It is the who, the how and the why which are different. In Shaping Our Lives, we all identify as disabled people or service users; that is to say, people eligible for (even if sometimes denied) the long-term health and social care support associated with our status as service users/disabled people. We also identify as a diverse group of service users, including older people, people with learning difficulties, those with long-term and/or life limiting conditions, people with sensory impairments and mental health service users/survivors.

For example, some people have speech and others hearing impairments, some are blind and need information in particular forms; because of this, we have placed a strong emphasis on making the way we work together as accessible and equal as possible. There are two people with learning difficulties on our management board and we work hard to keep our meetings, our process and our language clear and accessible, so these board members can have a real and equal say. They also have an expert supporter with them at and before such meetings, available to help them prepare. We also work hard to work in equal and respectful ways to each other. This means, for example, that you can't just add information at the last minute, as this will exclude many people who can't simply pick it up and read it, but may need time to go through it with voice technology or the assistance of a supporter. For us, how committed other organisations are to work in such accessible ways has become one of our acid tests of whether we want to collaborate with them. Sadly, for whatever reason, some that 'talk the talk' are still unable to 'walk the walk'.

Over the years, we have developed ground rules in Shaping Our Lives to guide how we work together and how we can behave in as accessible, inclusive and equal ways as possible. Someone volunteers to read these out at the beginning of each meeting, we agree them, and doing this helps shape our pace and focus us on what we are doing. For me at least, it helps calm me down. When we had one meeting with a funder present, they reported back later dismissively that it felt like a prayer meeting doing this, but it works for us! One thing that should be said, although this means that we may do things slowly, carefully and with an accent on keeping things clear and simple, we almost invariably get through all our business, something that is not necessarily true of all business meetings. At one meeting, one of the people with learning difficulties on the board summed up how we try and work together, in human and equal ways: "We are friends here, but we aren't just friends, we are colleagues." This emphasises how we seek to behave in kind, equal and respectful ways to each other, but we are also in a working, professional situation, accountable and must take responsibility for what we do as we are a formally constituted organisation, responsible for public money and to the people we seek to serve.

Of course we can have problems. We are only human too. But as well as seeking to work in human and inclusive ways, we have also recognised the importance of formal democratic processes and structures to deal with difficulties. So we have worked to combine such processes for resolving problems with our humanistic commitment to participatory democracy. This has included, over the years, bringing in an external consultant with relevant experience when we have felt we couldn't sort ourselves out on our own, as well as turning to formal consultations, investigations and appeals when there have been staff and board problems. Such processes have to be adapted to work in a truly inclusive way, but work they can. And all of us take responsibility to be involved in them; no one is excluded. Arrangements for formal and informal democracy, for participatory and more traditional democracy, do not have to be at odds with each other, but they do need to be related and connected to each other.

The importance of doing things differently

Even where the disabled people's movement has taken conventional direct action, by the very nature of being disabled people, it has had to do so in different ways and this has had different ramifications, which have had their own significance for its effectiveness. Thus one of the first highly visible examples of direct action taken by the disabled people's movement, through the Direct Action Network was to protest about the inaccessibility of London's Routemaster buses. Disabled people, including wheelchair users, chained themselves to buses, and sat and lay down around buses preventing them from moving (Campbell and Oliver, 1996). This created initial problems and uncertainties for the authorities, who were used to seeing disabled people as vulnerable people who needed help and were reluctant to respond in the same way as they would with non-disabled people. Subsequently, frustration and practical pressures meant that they sometimes behaved more aggressively, dragging disabled people about on the ground, pulling them out of wheelchairs and putting them in cells unsuited to their toilet and other needs. Both responses, of course, could play to the advantage of disabled protesters; either making conventional policing less effective or making it appear unduly aggressive and harsh. Thus again by having to work in different ways, disabled people and their organisations have created new opportunities for themselves, and new difficulties and understanding for those they challenge.

Finally, we must remember that, in how we do things in our organisations, we should work hard to avoid mirroring the old exclusions, the old hierarchies, the old inequalities, the old unkind practices. If we fail to keep these values in mind, we will end up as just another exclusionary clique, laying the ground perhaps for our own success and dominance, but not for the values of participation we have said we stand for. The idea of inclusive involvement is about working equally with people in different groups; groups which are both familiar and unfamiliar, groups you may feel comfortable or uncomfortable with. It is likely to mean working with new patterns of relationships, in culturally different ways, challenging, not reinforcing inequalities and hierarchies. All this is possible but potentially counter-intuitive and unfamiliar. Reversing traditional 'power over' and 'power under' relationships is not the same as getting rid of them. Inclusive involvement will be challenging for us all, even if ultimately more productive and rewarding for us all. And how well we are making the first real steps towards it will be revealed in how we seek to work together and treat each other in what we do.

8

Key concepts for participatory ideology

> Our greatness lies not so much in being able to remake the world ... as in being able to remake ourselves.
>
> Mahatma Gandhi,
> South African/Indian activist, undated

Ultimately, participation is a practical act. As the sociologist Carole Pateman wrote: 'The evidence supports the arguments of Rousseau, [John Stuart] Mill and [G.D.H.] Cole that we ... learn to participate by participating and that feelings of political efficacy are more likely to be developed in a participatory environment' (Pateman, 1970, p 105). Yet it is also closely bound up with theory and theory-based concepts. Participation and political ideology are not only big ideas in their own right. Each also, as we have seen, draws us to and needs to be considered in relation to other key concepts. These include for example, concepts and issues of power, diversity and discrimination – all of which we have already encountered in this discussion. We now turn to three others – all critical if we are to make the connections between participation and ideology. These are empowerment, language and knowledge. As well as being key in conceptual analysis, they are also, of course, central to taking forward participatory ideology itself. That isn't to say that there aren't more such issues, or that other people may not have different lists. The point being made here is that these seem especially important from embarking on this project and need to be given serious attention if our commitment is to participatory ideology, particularly inclusive involvement in ideology, and achieving it. In this chapter, we will be focusing on these three ideas/issues and the part they may play in bringing about this different kind of participatory ideology.

This leads us to questions around change and making change. Change is at the heart of this book; changing our understanding of political ideology, changing our roles and relationships with it and changing our assumptions about both ourselves and the wider worlds we live in. All three issues and concepts we are discussing here are at the heart of making change. Even more to the point, here we are concerned with a different model for making change – a participatory model and key ideas which lie at the heart of it. This is therefore a good place to engage with the literature and theorising on social change, as a helpful foundation for this discussion.

Theorising social change

The aim of moving from an imposed and exclusionary understanding of and approaches to political ideology represents a massive change. Change is a key sociological concept. Sociologists have identified many forms of change, including behavioural, organisational, social, economic, cultural, ideological and political change (Haralambos and Holborn, 2008; Vago, 2019). Social change may be driven through cultural, religious, economic, scientific or technological forces (Giddens and Sutton, 2017). As we have seen, when mainstream commentators discuss ideological change, they have primarily been concerned with changes in the aims and purpose of ideology, not its exclusionary processes.

There are both different theories about making social change and different locations where these are explored. In recent UK social policy, for example, there has been a tendency to focus explicitly on organisational change, while fundamental ideological change has been taking place. Some theoreticians have explored the interrelations between assumptions about human motivation and public policy. Julian Le Grand, for instance, as we saw earlier, highlighted the move from ideas based on individual altruism which underpinned the creation of the original UK welfare state, to beliefs assuming people's innate selfishness, linked with the shift to market-led welfare (Le Grand, 1997).

Paul Watzlawick, the therapist, and others distinguished between two forms of change – *first order change*, as incremental change within a system, and *second order change*, changing the system itself. That has a bearing on this discussion, where we are clearly talking about the latter (Watzlawick et al, 1974).

While existing power holders may want to avoid change that they see as threatening, welfare service user and other new social movements are generally committed to *liberatory* change. This leads us to the first of the ideas we will explore in this chapter – *empowerment* – as they seek to make connections between individual understandings and broader policy and politics (Arches and Fleming, 2006). Change here is part of a broader agenda for challenging oppression and securing people's civil and human rights (Oliver, 1990; 2009).

While, as has been helpfully argued, 'no one person or group can expect to be in control of all the many factors that will affect change' (Smale, 1998, p 321), key individuals and groups can play a disproportionate role. This brings us back to the issue of power, the distribution and location of power and the relative power of different stakeholders in any process of making change – or resisting it. This issue is particularly apparent where change is imposed. Then the experience of change for people in control is likely to be significantly different to those on the receiving end of such change. The latter may be even further disempowered by their own lack of experience in exerting power. This again raises the issue of people's differential capacity to use what power they may have and the need for support to do so, especially in the context of change-making (Fleming and Ward, 2004).

Different approaches to conceptualising social change have been developed which can be helpful for us here. One draws a distinction between *externally imposed* and *internally adapted* change. In UK health policy, for example, the former has been associated with frequent reorganisations and restructuring, disrupting the lives of both workers and patients; the latter with micro-level change mediated by workers and sensitive to the needs of service users (Beresford et al, 2011, pp 363–4; Cheng, 2012, pp 157 and following).

Another related approach draws a distinction between *top-down* and *bottom-up* change. Here the first essentially imposes change in a hierarchical way on those who must work and live with it, while the second is presented as coming from the grassroots, originating and owned by the people on the ground. While the reality is likely to be more complex (and this author has certainly encountered approaches which are some kind of meld of bottom-up and top-down), the typology is helpful because it highlights the origin of pressure for change and the possible implications this may have (Beresford et al, 2011).

Certainly this last approach seems particularly relevant to our focus in this book – a participatory approach to political ideology. This is the essence of bottom-up. But more than that, perhaps, is to understand our focus here as the emergence of a *different paradigm* in relation to political ideology, its conceptualisation and implementation.

The US philosopher of science, Thomas S. Kuhn, introduced the idea of 'paradigm shift', arguing that scientific understanding and ideas do not progress solely in a linear and continuous way but also undergo periodic fundamental changes or 'paradigm shifts' as he called it (Kuhn, 1970). Hidden assumptions, beliefs, habits of mind and action, influence how we see and do things. What we can infer from this is that what might be needed is not another ideology or model or theory of ideology, but a wholly different approach to ideology, based on a different process and on different knowledges and ways of understanding.

This book has been concerned with exploring and taking forward just such a paradigm shift – one based on inclusive participation. This appears to represent a fundamental break with traditional thinking on ideology, since it is no longer concerned with power holders or 'experts' advancing and imposing their different ideas and proposals. This book highlights both the need for and possibility of developing political ideology in which we as service users, workers and other citizens have a real say and involvement at an analytic, structural and socio-political level. It highlights the need to focus on more than just the struggle of individuals to exercise their individual citizen, social and welfare rights, suggesting that if we do so these struggles are much more likely to be successful. Such a methodology isn't just concerned with a different approach to the process and structures of political ideology. It also offers the basis for the *development* of different kinds of analysis and different theory.

This is concerned with supporting the democratisation of political ideology by giving priority to people's own lived experience and their central involvement in taking forward such ideology. Kuhn argued that rival paradigms are incommensurable – that is, it is not possible to understand one paradigm through the conceptual framework and terminology of another rival paradigm. This helps us to understand both why the exponents of traditional discourse haven't significantly valued the participatory approaches advanced, for example, by disabled people and their organisations and the resulting limitations of their critiques. As Kuhn says, 'the transfer of allegiance from one paradigm to another is a conversion experience that cannot be forced' (Kuhn, 1970, pp 198–204). This is the kind of epiphany that millions of disabled people and other service users have undergone, as they have come together, organised, shared their experience and developed their own ideas and alternatives – as we have seen in this book. This brings us back to the key concepts we now want to explore, all of which are central to shifting to this different paradigm.

Empowerment

The first of these, empowerment, is crucial for any process of inclusive participatory change. It has the capacity as an idea to connect us with our political selves; to bring together the personal and the political and put them in positive relation with each other. It can be and often has been misused and devalued as a concept, so we need to start with a health warning. But that is no reason to shy away from all the help and insights the idea of empowerment has to offer. We should see it for what it is at heart: a two-fold concept that is connected by a two-way relationship, which links the personal and the political; the individual and the collective. Because of this, it is just too important to ignore.

However, to begin with we have to make clear that there is no overall agreement about the meaning of empowerment. Many different strands can be identified in the idea's development and usage. Empowerment theory has roots in Marxist sociological theory as well as US community psychology. There have been managerialist, self-help, liberational, professional and market models of empowerment (Shera and Wells, 1999). These are in complex relationship with each other. While there are some overlaps between them, there are also important differences.

Professional interest in empowerment has developed in response to the new demands of consumerist approaches to public policy. It has, for example, been trivialised by global cosmetics companies selling their products on the promise of 'empowering' women. The idea of empowerment has been used to individualise but also to renew collective action. It was the signature organising concept of the US Black civil rights movement. It has worked as a force for change for new social movements, seeking to equip people to become activists, rather than using them passively to make up the numbers. Here we are not ignoring its vulnerability to being subverted and minimised, but we are focusing instead on its particular strength as an idea that can truly engage people in being involved in making broader political and social change.

Unifying the personal and political

In this author's view, this is because empowerment is in essence, as we have said, a two-part idea; an idea that focuses on us and our capacity to be active participants and the worlds in which we may do this. It is therefore a truly sociological idea, in the sense that C. Wright Mills talked about sociological imagination, because in its duality, it engages with both our individual biography and the history in which we are situated (Mills, 1959). What is special about it is the way it has been used to reunite individual biography and history and offers a praxis for reuniting the two.

Enabling personal change

Both aspects of the idea of empowerment are about making change. First, as developed by progressive campaigners, it is concerned with the making of personal change. It is about us making changes in ourselves, so we are able to explore our relation with each other and the wider world so we can then change these in order to impact more effectively together on the wider world. So empowerment is first about personal reflection, review and revision. It is about how we can rethink ourselves as active agents in our lives and worlds, rather than how we may have been taught to think of ourselves, as passive and powerless objects who may hope for good luck and opportunities, but recognise that they are more at the beck and call of more powerful forces which they have very limited capacity to influence or challenge. So in the 1950s many people put their faith in football pools as the route to change their lives. Now it is the national and other lotteries.

In contrast, personal empowerment is, for example, about:

- recognising and questioning the negative identities and discrimination we have sometimes had imposed on us;
- learning ways of rethinking ourselves and what we are capable of;
- getting a better understanding of our situation and what is happening to us;
- gaining new knowledge and skills and being able to value our own experience and knowledge and those of other people in similar situations;
- recognising from others with shared experience that we don't have to see ourselves in negative terms, as the problem, to blame for what happens to us;
- challenging negative views and stereotypes of people with our experience and identities and developing our own understandings of ourselves;
- increasing our self-confidence, assertiveness and preparedness to do new things and take on fresh challenges;
- recognising that we have the potential to try and make change;
- learning how to work with others for change.

Thus, key to personal empowerment are reflection and reflexivity – and opportunities and spurs for both.

This list is a personal one for starters. Others will doubtless have more and different things to add. But the point is that unless we start from circumstances where from an early age we have been socialised to see and understand ourselves as active political beings (and the more privileged among us clearly are nurtured to be more in that position, perpetuating inequalities), then we have to acquire these understandings, skills and states of mind. They put us at the starting point to be political actors. Everything else is just making up the numbers, rather than exerting real agency. Getting to this point will almost certainly demand either outside assistance or some major change or happening that presses us towards a rethink. The value of the idea of empowerment is that it serves to articulate this; that being an active and effective citizen is not necessarily a natural state for everyone, that some face particular barriers achieving it; that it is a journey many of us never really embark upon and which we need support to be aware of and to undertake. Equally, there are others who, because of some injustice or awful tragedy in their life, are forced to undergo a crash course in empowerment. And, while the idea of empowerment is usually associated with particular groups experiencing disempowerment, exclusions and discriminations, in truth in many societies, including the UK, many, many people and groups are marginalised in and by political processes. That personal empowerment is all our business is a point made through history by those who have been fortunate enough to learn the lesson themselves. Thus:

> 'Life is not easy for any of us. But what of that? We must have perseverance and above all confidence in ourselves. We must believe that we are gifted for something and that this thing must be attained.' Marie Curie, scientist (quoted in Philosiblog, 2013)

> 'Always be a first-rate version of yourself, instead of a second-rate version of somebody else.' Judy Garland, film star (quoted in Kennedy, 1992)

> 'The most common way people give up their power is by thinking they don't have any.' Alice Walker, African-American novelist (quoted in Martin, 2004)

Participation unsupported by a process of empowerment is unlikely to lead to progressive change. The two are in complex and potentially interlocking relationship. Thus personal empowerment can equip people to deal effectively with opportunities for collective involvement. As we have already indicated, without it, they are at serious risk of being tyrannised by token arrangements for their involvement (Cooke and Kothari, 2001; Hickey and Mohan, 2004).

A basis for political change

While personal empowerment is a necessary part of a process of participation, it is not enough on its own. However, it can inspire us to be part of getting involved in and working for progressive political and ideological change. Thus Gandhi inspired change in people that in turn could make it possible for them to struggle for political change against all odds and in the face of extreme violence (Miller, 1936). We must remember though that he and they were unable to secure the fundamental political transformation he ultimately sought,. However they were at least able to be truly involved in seeking it. The concept of *conscientisation*, created by the philosopher activist Paulo Freire, is closely connected with the idea of empowerment. He used it to mean a process of developing a critical awareness of one's social reality through reflection and action. This embraces the two aspects of empowerment and is another reminder of the importance of both (Freire, 1972).

And that leads us to the second aspect or dimension of the idea of empowerment. This is working to bring about political, social and other change. Here it means actively seeking to exercise power to achieve your goals. Personal empowerment helps put you in a position to take more control over your own life – as an individual. But crucially it extends to processes that make it more possible for you to try and exert more influence beyond yourself – particularly in association with others. So it highlights a pre-requisite for effective, meaningful *collective action* for change; that the individual is personally equipped consciously to be part of a process of making such change. This is very different to being driven in desperation to be part of a mob, which feels it has little alternative than to aim its bodies against the status quo, or to be manipulated to be part of someone else's stage army to fight on their behalf. So often the two aspects of empowerment – its personal and political aspects – are apart, separated, divorced; their relationship unexplored and ignored as though being a political being is something that comes naturally and is widely understood.

The idea of empowerment helps us to understand that participation in political processes require us both to have particular internal understandings and states of mind about what we can do, as well as opportunities, particularly alongside others, to do it. Such ways of working for political empowerment to bring about change can take many forms; the forms we are familiar with from other discussions of campaigning, collective action and so on. The tactics and strategies are not necessarily special or unique. They can include:

- community development approaches
- campaigning
- direct action
- educational approaches
- faith-based approaches (as, for example, in the Black civil rights movement)

What is specific about them in relation to understandings of empowerment is our relation with them and the attention paid to making them inclusive and culturally appropriate. We make the decisions about how we will try and take forward our collective action; we play an active part in shaping and deciding on the forms and processes we use. These are not simply chosen or imposed on us by other people – by external leaders who may not share or even value our experience.

A straightforward definition of empowerment, and one which conveys this dualistic understanding of the idea as adopted by new social movements, is set out by Wikipedia: 'The term empowerment refers to measures designed to increase the degree of autonomy and self-determination in people and in communities in order to enable them to represent their interests in a responsible and self-determined way, acting on their own authority' (https://en.wikipedia.org/wiki/Empowerment). While ideas of empowerment seem to underpin all new social movements to some degree or other, whether explicit or not, as previously noted, they played a particularly important and explicit role in the US Black civil rights movement of the 1950s and 1960s. As one resource guide discussing education for empowerment states:

> It makes sense to make empowerment a central theme and focus when teaching about the civil rights movement. Without it, the movement makes little sense ... Empowerment begins by teaching students to think critically about history and to question the conventional story and seek the story beneath. Critical thinking includes examining the common ways in which historical fact is created and presented. As Ohio State University professor Beverly M. Gordon writes, students 'question what is not being said as well as what is stated'. The civil rights movement offers many opportunities to question assumptions and poke holes in the conventional narrative. An excellent example, and promising first lesson, is told in

Herbert Kohl's famous essay 'Rosa [Parks] was tired ...'. Here, the widely accepted, and false, story of Rosa Parks is unravelled in favor of a more truthful and more complicated version that shows Rosa Parks as a dedicated activist whose resistance was planned. (www.tolerance. org/magazine/publications/the-march-continues/ the-five-essential-practices-for-teaching-the-civil)

One further point needs to be made. People can be *supported* to become more empowered, but *we can only empower ourselves*. It is a contradiction in terms for one group of people to see themselves as empowering another. Power cannot be given, it can only be taken. This point was famously made by Gloria Steinem, the feminist activist we encountered earlier, who said: 'Power can be taken, but not given. The process of the taking is empowerment in itself' (Steinem, 2012, p 577).

There have been modern attempts to frame some helping professions, for example, social work, in terms of empowering people (Stevenson and Parsloe, 1993). There is an irony here, given that social work is one of the most devalued and marginalised professions, with a serious and expanding social control role. Such professionals can play a helpful role in supporting people to empower themselves by offering the opportunities, insights and circumstances for this to happen, but any suggestion that they can act as 'empowerers' themselves demonstrates a failure to understand the true essential nature of the idea as one based on change from within.

Working together in our own organisations provides the ideal conditions to support people's empowerment. Like the concept of empowerment itself, such conditions address the two key elements required for effective and inclusive involvement. These are the conditions and prerequisites for personal growth and development and meaningful opportunities to take collective action for change. Thus user-led organisations offer their members:

- chances to learn from others with shared histories and experiences how they can rethink themselves – who they are, why this is and what may be possible for them as a starting point for getting involved;
- chances to take collective action with others with common concerns and objectives, to realise a commitment to involvement in change.

Thus they provide a critical platform for the reunification of the two aspects of empowerment, a resource for advancing personal empowerment while at the same time an opportunity and force for collectivity. In this author's view, no other platform offers such a promising starting point for collective empowerment and change.

Language

We have already touched in Chapter 3 on the importance of language for ideology and seen how it is used to advance certain ideologies and in turn can be shaped by dominant ideologies. The meaning of almost every word is shaped by its ideological relations. Thus the word freedom in the context of Right-wing ideology tends to mean *freedom to* – to do what you like without being constrained to safeguard the rights of others. From a Left-wing perspective, it is more likely to mean *freedom from* – from want, abuse and social injustice.

Any discussion of ideology and participation in ideology must also address language, just as any discussion of language must address ideology. Yet we tend to take language for granted and treat it as unproblematic. But we will be wise to heed cautions not to do this. Warnings come from many sources, from philosophers to poets, for example:

> For last year's words belong to last year's language
> And next year's words await another voice.
>> T.S. Eliot, poet, *Four Quartets* (Eliot, 2001, first
>> published 1941)

> But if thought corrupts language, language can also corrupt thought.
>> George Orwell, essayist and novelist,
>> *Nineteen Eighty-Four* (Orwell, 1949)

> The limits of my language means the limits of my world.
>> Ludwig Wittgenstein, philosopher
>> (Wittgenstein, 2013,[1921])

Close relations exist between language and ideology. As one commentator has put it:

> The relationship of language and ideology is so ingrained and basic that it would be difficult to see them operate in isolation from each other. It is through the combine of language and ideology that status quo is maintained in

society and truths and falsehoods spread and crystallized. As can be understood from examples collected by some of the foremost voices of our time, the transformative power of language of ideology or ideology of language is vast, strong, and lasting. (Zaidi, 2012, p 71)

Language and inequality

Thus colonial powers marginalise or even criminalise indigenous languages. Particular languages, for example, Latin in the Roman Catholic church, are used to mystify or give special authority to official pronouncements. Vocabularies are manipulated to support the aims and objectives of ruling ideologies.

As we saw earlier, George Orwell was one of the first writers to examine the relationship between language and ideology. In his 1946 essay 'Politics and the English Language', he wrote: 'political speech and writing are largely the defence of the indefensible ... Thus political language has to consist largely of euphemism, question-begging and sheer cloudy vagueness' (Orwell, 2013, p 7). More recently Noam Chomsky, the philosopher and activist, discussing how language is employed in the service of ideology, has argued that:

> from the Cold War onwards the United States has been interfering in every part of the world in the name of human rights and democracy, but in fact these interventions are meant to destroy indigenous oppositions to American exploitation. In Asia, Africa, and Latin America, the United States has promoted highly emotive theses such as 'human rights' and 'crimes against humanity' in order to demonize anti-American resistance. (Zaidi, 2012, p 80)

Language is regularly used to disguise the meaning and direction of ideology. If, as we have argued, ideology is an idea that many of us may not feel familiar with or able to define or discuss adequately, language on the other hand is something we are much more likely to feel comfortable with and simply to take for granted. The sense of safety afforded is often deceptive and illusory. Thus it is easy to come at language uncritically accepting the language we have been taught or socialised into. But, of course, as commentators like those cited make clear, language is an ideological battlefield. Language can and does influence and shape:

- how we think;
- how we think about other people and groups;
- our preparedness to follow certain leads and take particular actions.

Language and power

Language is indeed powerful and far from neutral. It can be used to tell us what we should and shouldn't think; how we should see ourselves and others; what is good and bad, right or wrong. Language can be used to:

- encourage and perpetuate certain attitudes and assumptions;
- disguise intent or effect and serve as a euphemism;
- encourage oppression and discrimination against particular groups and people.

Language has long been used to glorify war and convert it rhetorically from a mass meat grinder of horror and terror to something individual, noble and inspirational. Thus globally generations of little boys continue to become eager recruits to 'test their mettle', leading many to pointless cruelty, mutilation and slaughter. Our uncertainties about the unknown are converted into fear and hatred of the foreigner with the creation of terms like 'asylum seeker' and 'economic refugee' by self-seeking politicians like Theresa May, Nigel Farage and Boris Johnson.

Language can be used to keep power and control where it is. Equally if we want to challenge that state of affairs, it is likely we will have to challenge the language we have been socialised into and which we have internalised. One of the early tasks that the members of new social movements based around identity and shared experience took on was to challenge the language used about them and develop their own terminology for themselves. Sometimes, as part of this challenge, they sought to reclaim terms intended to demean and degrade them, like 'dyke', 'crip' and 'mad'. Almost invariably they generated new understandings for and about themselves, as for instance, we saw earlier with the disabled people's movement and terms like independence and disability.

People generating their own languages and meanings can be seen as a sign and signal of them seeking to subvert imposed ideologies and developing ownership of their own. Developing our own language in this way can be seen as part of the process of participating in the development of ideology; with a renewed language based on respect, equality, inclusion and social justice, reflecting the values that emancipatory organisations and movements prioritise.

As has already been suggested here, we must also remember that language is much more than the written word. And this is particularly true in relation to ideology, where much is about the power of persuasion, of suggestibility and of rhetoric. Political ideology is crucially about engaging with people's emotions as well as their intellect. Great orators have always had significance from ancient Greece and Rome onwards, but until the 20th century people could only be heard as far as their voice would carry or through written texts by the limited number who could read. Perhaps this coupling of ideology with the rise of mass communication helps explain why the 20th century became the epoch of mass ideological innovation and impact.

Similarly, we should be aware that technology is not neutral and therefore that it tends primarily to serve the interests of power holders rather than the disempowered. This can be a difficult lesson to learn, so that the advent of the internet, the world wide web and social media was initially heralded as a major challenge to the power of traditional media, summed up in the importance attributed to these new platforms during the 'Arab Spring' and international student protests. Now in the age of Google, Facebook, Johnson, Trumpism and 'fake news', the dark net, Cambridge Analytica and its successors, we can discern a much more complex and ambiguous scenario. Nonetheless politicians and their speeches, drawing on long established techniques, continue to shape narratives and debates, sometimes explicitly, sometimes imperceptibly changing their terms and leaving us on the outside of their disguised meanings (Atkinson, 1984; Fairclough, 2000).

Making language explicit

Such discussions of language are important, although we should also recognise that they can be used as a diversion. We can end up spending so much time analysing the language we use and our different preferences that we lose sight of our primary focus – working for change. Some of those resisting our efforts to make real change, as the pioneering social work activist David Brandon once said, are also 'good at talking the talk', even if they are reluctant 'to walk the walk'. So, while those seeking to challenge dominant ideologies and their associated language are concerned with renewing language and meanings, those they challenge are equally committed to undermining these. Thus new terms and ideas like 'peer support', 'self advocacy', 'direct payments' and the 'recovery model' are fed back to their originators, the disabled people's and mental health service users'/survivors' movement, subverted and divested of their intended meaning by the ruling service system. This is a constant struggle, which causes confusion and division.

We need to interrogate and analyse the dominant languages that we are subjected to. We need to monitor our own internalisation of them. It can be really helpful, as the disabled people's/service users' organisation and network does that this author is part of, to offer our own unambiguous definitions of what we mean by the key terms we use.

We may only know the oppressor's language and so it continues to oppress us. We may not have an agreed and common language of our own and this acts as a serious barrier to change. We may not realise that the dominant ideology uses the same words as us but for very different reasons and with different meanings and intentions. We must learn to be generous where people with shared goals use different language and to try and avoid language that is painful for others or is being used to divide us. We should remember that we might have shared values and concerns even if we have not yet developed a common language and vocabulary. Language is both something that we develop as part of the strengthening of our collectivity and something which signifies this.

Knowledge

Over time key voices as diverse as those of the physicist Albert Einstein and the educator Paulo Freire have highlighted the importance of experiential knowledge and of people being able to make their own enquiries:

> Any situation in which some men [sic] prevent others from engaging in the process of inquiry is one of violence; ... to alienate humans from their own decision making is to change them into objects. (Freire, 1972)

> The only source of knowledge is experience. (Einstein, undated)

Ideologies tend to be presented as having their own body of knowledge. That knowledge is seen as providing an ideology's authority and validity. There has been a tendency for modern political ideologies to emphasise their 'scientific' credentials and that of the knowledge upon which they are based. This extends from the phoney science used in Nazi Germany to give credibility to theories of Aryanism to the efforts made by UK Fabian theorists from the early 20th century to justify their approach to social policy as scientific, which extended to many even advocating eugenics. The political theorist and philosopher Hannah Arendt wrote: 'an ideology differs from a simple opinion in that it claims to possess either the key to history, or the solution for all the "riddles of the universe", or the intimate knowledge of the hidden universal laws, which are supposed to rule nature and man [sic]' (Arendt, 1968, p 159).

Narrowing the knowledge basis

Like most ideologies, such ideologically related knowledge tends to be narrowly owned and based. We generally have to sign up to other people's ideologies and accept their evidential base for them. Yet there is often also a pretence that the knowledge base is everyone's: that there is consensus about this underpinning and ruling knowledge. As the revolutionary Black philosopher Frantz Fanon argued colonisation is not just physical, there is also colonisation of the mind, as the knowledge (and indeed language) of the coloniser is imposed on the colonised to internalise the belief that they are inferior (Fanon, 1967).

This draws us back to our starting point. Our present discussion has its origins in the earlier exploration of the ownership of knowledge in the short pamphlet, *It's Our Lives* (Beresford, 2003). We need now to return to that to take up our story about the democratisation of ideology. It's not surprising that where ideologies are imposed and controlling, their knowledge base is similarly restricted. On the other hand, if we are working towards more participatory ideology, then it is only to be expected that we will need to find ways to ensure that its knowledge base is broader, more inclusive – more participatory.

The present situation reflects broader processes of exclusion in knowledge production. Put more simply, some knowledge is granted more value than others; the knowledge of some is granted more credibility than that of others. Some 'knowledge claims' are seen as more valid than others. Terms like 'epistemic injustice' and 'epistemic violence' have been coined to highlight the devaluing of some knowledge and some people's knowledge. The philosopher Miranda Fricker has argued that there is a distinctively epistemic type of injustice where someone is wronged specifically in their capacity as a 'knower' (Fricker, 2007). This is associated with inequalities of power and discrimination.

Four years earlier in *It's Our Lives* (which interestingly was not mentioned in the academic discussion about epistemic injustice cited) I had tried to explore some of the ways in which processes and structures of knowledge production seemed to discriminate against those facing some of the worst disempowerment and oppression (Beresford, 2003).

I began by highlighting that 'knowledge', like ideology, is one of those 'big', portentous words that many people may not often think about and which can be intimidating when you do. Perhaps because knowledge is a complicated word, it is often talked about in complicated ways. Long words like 'epistemology' and 'ontology' tend to get used, which can make discussion even more excluding. Since the 19th century particularly, there has been an emphasis on science and 'being scientific' in knowledge production. Paradoxically the word science has its origins in the Latin *scio, scientes* – which means no more than *knowing*. With their emphasis on science and being scientific, post Enlightenment approaches to knowledge were based on the idea that you could best find out about people, how they lived and the societies they lived in, in the same way that you could find out about the natural world, through experiment and measurement. An emphasis developed on particular 'scientific' values, the most important of these were values of neutrality, objectivity and distance;

- neutrality – meaning not being biased about something, through being involved in any way – being detached and without any vested interest;
- objective – meaning not being influenced or affected by feelings or opinions – being able to consider something coolly, dispassionately, without being emotionally or personally involved;
- distance – meaning not being close to the subject under consideration, being able to 'see the big picture', and not being affected by it.

All these values emphasise that the person who is the 'knower' is likely to have the strongest 'knowledge claims' if they are unaffected by, separated and distant from the subject of their attention, that is, what they know or are trying to find out about. But there is a worrying aspect to this conventional approach to estimating the value of different knowledges, one which raises important issues for developing the knowledge base of ideologies.

We have seen how the ownership of ideologies has generally been limited and that they tend to be accepted or imposed on the many by the few. The kind of conventional approach to knowledge development discussed previously mirrors and reinforces such an inequality of power and ownership, rather than challenging it. To appreciate this, just think of the people and groups who are either especially likely to want to challenge and reject dominant ideologies or to develop alternative liberatory ideologies of their own. In both cases they can be expected to have experience of oppression, exclusion and discrimination. As we have seen, if you have such direct experience, then what you say and know will always be seen as having less value – less credibility. This is because you will be seen as 'close to the problem' – it directly affects you ,you cannot claim that you are 'neutral', 'objective' and 'distant' from it.

Challenging knowledge discrimination

So here is the key point. On top of the discrimination and oppression you may already experience, you face an additional problem. You can expect to be seen as a less reliable source of knowledge, an inferior 'knower'. If you seek to challenge an ideology's body of knowledge, or be involved in the development of other knowledge to underpin an emerging ideology you espouse, then your 'knowledge claim' will be regarded and treated as inferior. There's a double problem here too. It's not only that the knowledge of people who experience oppression and exclusion is likely to be given less value and credibility where values of neutrality, objectivity and distance rule. Such values privilege those who don't have such first-hand experience because they in contrast can claim to be 'objective', 'impartial' and distanced. In this way, their ignorance is seen to make them better 'knowers' or sources of knowledge. It adds to the power that they are already likely to have over those who face disempowerment and helps them keep control of both ideology and associated knowledge. What this tends to mean is that the knowledge(s) of those seeking liberation from oppression is likely to be regarded as having less validity than that of those who control ideology, who we can expect both to have more power and be granted greater legitimacy. Thus traditional approaches to the production of knowledge reinforce the powerlessness of people with little power and help perpetuate their exclusion and marginalisation in the social production of ideology.

Once they began to realise that their knowledges were not given equal weight in their societies, groups facing discrimination and exclusion sought to challenge the barriers they face by developing their own research. Women, Black people and members of other ethnic groups, and LGBTQ people have all done this. In so doing, as part of new social movements, they have pioneered innovative and groundbreaking approaches to research, generating more emancipatory and participatory approaches and new forms of and focuses for knowledge. This has also been true of some of the most marginalised groups and communities, including, for example, disabled people and mental health service users/survivors, as we have seen.

They have developed a significant and growing body of research projects and findings as well as new research approaches and new relations with change-making. However, over the years, it has also become increasingly apparent that their user-led/user-controlled research, just like their individual and collective experiential knowledge, faces major barriers and exclusions (Beresford, 2019a; Carr, 2019). This has increasingly been reflected, as well as documented, in their unequal and inferior access to funding support, the problems they face undertaking major research projects, and the barriers they face in getting their findings published, securing research training and mainstream research jobs.

At the same time, there is continuing official, state and research interest in what has come to be called in the UK PPI/PPIE, or 'public and patient involvement and engagement'. But this increasingly seems an ambiguous development. Service user researchers have increasingly been highlighting that such involvement is often limited, tokenistic and retrograde. Control remains with traditional researchers and their organisations and the involvement is often just a tick-box exercise only allowed to operate within conventional research and policy parameters rather than being encouraged to challenge them. Getting involved in the structures of PPI, therefore, can be damaging, ineffective and feel very non-participative. But equally, where there is a desire among researchers to be genuinely open and participative, it can be positive and rewarding. If there is a lesson to be learned from this, it is that a twin track approach to challenging epistemic injustice and advancing the cause of experiential knowledge is likely to be based both on developing our own research and knowledge and entering and influencing formal opportunities for involvement in the processes of ruling knowledge production, wherever possible (Beresford, 2019a; Carr, 2019).

Democratising knowledge

Unless we challenge traditional approaches to knowledge development, they will continue to be a major barrier in the way of opening up ownership of and the democratisation of ideology. We have to recognise this problem if we are successfully to challenge it. Such a campaign of 'epistemic resistance', as Jose Medina has described it, needs to be an essential element in any strategy to democratise ideology as a basis for achieving greater social justice. Medina defines such resistance as: 'the use of our epistemic resources and abilities to undermine and change oppressive normative structures and the complacent cognitive-affective functioning that sustains those structures' (Medina, 2012). As the French researcher Roberto Frega has written: 'Epistemic resistance is clearly a political act, as it is addressed against injustices that are embedded in social relations' (Frega, 2013). As part of that resistance it is also important to challenge the assumptions and theory-building that have perpetuated inequality in knowledge production historically. *It's Our Lives* offered a hypothesis around which to frame this (Beresford, 2003). Positivist research and knowledge production have rested on the belief that the greater the distance between direct experience and knowledge, then the more likely it is that knowledge will be reliable and accurate. Here it is suggested that the shorter the distance between experience and its interpretation then the *more* reliable and accurate resulting knowledge is likely to be. The author believes that this can offer a rallying point both for reclaiming the value and validity of our own experiential knowledge and for gaining greater control of the knowledge base of the causes and ideologies we seek to advance.

Democratising knowledge for participatory ideology

The importance of gaining greater control of the knowledge base of the causes and ideologies we seek to advance has been a key lesson. It has certainly been the lesson learned from the new social movements emerging during the latter part of the 20th century. It wasn't until the emergence of these movements of women, Black people, LGBTQ communities and disabled people, that traditional understandings of race, gender, sexuality and disability came under effective scrutiny and challenge and very different liberatory analyses and interpretations became the starting point for understanding, action and change. These movements also offered the opportunities for individual concerns to be subjected to collective scrutiny and the development of collective understandings and knowledge (Lent, 2002).

What is also important about them is that they bring into the arena of knowledge production perspectives, experience and sources of knowledge that have previously been excluded, reinterpreted or marginalised. We know from these movements that the inclusion of such erstwhile hidden knowledge can lead to the reshaping of ideology and the challenging of traditional assumptions and beliefs. That is why it is so important in this discussion of participatory ideology.

The knowledge democratisation movement

As we have been seeing, almost every aspect of knowledge and its production is associated with inequalities. This applies to the opportunities people have to learn and the value attached to what they know and their status as knowers. Education has long been recognised as a route to equalising opportunity and enabling greater equality, but with under-resourced state education and the private/public education split, it more often reinforces inequality. The perpetuation of such knowledge inequality has given rise to the knowledge democracy movement, which is based on the belief that social justice is inextricably bound up with knowledge democracy and environmental justice (Hall, 2011; Rowell and Feldman, 2019).

This movement pulls together a range of developments, like engaged scholarship, community-based research, strategies for knowledge exchange and transfer, knowledge mobilisation, and community-university research partnerships and engagements. This approach is explicitly committed to being action-orientated, seeing people's knowledge as part of a mobilising and organising strategy, and to supporting the struggles of disempowered peoples and groups. It highlights the importance of indigenous and racialised forms of knowledge and the knowledges of marginalised and oppressed groups.

But it also carries its own risks, which must be kept under close watch. While the knowledge democracy movement may represent a collective extension of challenging epistemic injustice, it can be a double-edged sword. Some of the research approaches associated with it, like 'participatory action research' and 'community-based (participatory) research', are treated with some suspicion by those on the receiving end.

While these first came in for criticism from advocates of traditional positivist research approaches, who dismissed them as ideologically biased and methodologically weak, they have also been called into question from more progressive perspectives. Their aspiration to involve research participants and support social justice is set against the limited degree to which they effectively achieve transfer of power from researcher to researched in their process and outcomes. CBR is a collaborative approach to research between academic researchers and communities that seeks to build on the strengths and assets of the partners and engender trust between them. As one commentator has put it, there is little 'hard data on the extent to which CBPR has led to community empowerment or reductions in poverty, but there are many anecdotal and case reports that suggest that the process of CBPR does, indeed, benefit communities' (Blumental, 2011, p 389). The perceived limitations of participatory action research have led to the development of 'critical participatory action research', which places an additional emphasis on the researcher engaging themselves in an ongoing process of self-reflection (Mackay, 2016).

While not all organisations identified with the global knowledge democracy movement are based in academia, its strong association with higher education and universities with their overall commitment to elitism puts it at risk of reinforcing inequalities and exclusions and taking control away from people (Ross et al, 2010). Such concerns have been raised in the context of Disability Studies and Mad Studies. This is particularly the case at a time when the imposition of neoliberal policy, practices and ideology has increasingly pressured universities internationally to be more competitive and self-funding in a market economy. But these developments also highlight a growing and significant concern to value and draw on different kinds and sources of knowledge without prejudice and to unite to advance an inclusive knowledge base for action and change. Thus such collaborations need to be based on true co-production if they are to address rather than increase the problems identified – and this can be more easily said than done.

9

Conclusion: reclaiming ideology

> The teacher is of course an artist, but being an artist does
> not mean that he or she can make the profile, can shape the
> students. What the educator does in teaching is to make it
> possible for the students to become themselves.
>
> Paulo Freire, *We Make the Road by*
> *Walking: Conversations on Education and*
> *Social Change*, quoted in Bell et al, 1990

A straightforward argument underpins and runs through this book.
Put simply, the suggestion is that the best way to develop ideas about
how to promote equality and freedom is to be involved in developing
those ideas together. The only way we are likely to achieve democratic
goals (ideology) is through democratic means (participation). To have
the desired effect, we must use the same method, that is, democratic
participation. We must do it together, equally and inclusively. If we
don't, if we follow the old exclusionary ways, the result is again likely
to be exclusionary ideology. Ideology in which we don't have an equal
involvement is invariably problematic because it cannot include and
reflect all our interests, experience, knowledges and perspectives. How
can it adequately address all our rights, responsibilities and entitlements?
It must privilege some, inevitably at the expense of others.

   Yet in our exploration of political ideology here, what has emerged is
that generally speaking, few of us have any real say in the ideologies that
operate on and shape us and our lives. This can be as true of counter-
ideologies challenging those that oppress us as of the latter themselves.
Different ideological perspectives are wielded by humans to explain, justify
and legitimise a political or social order. Ideologies are essentially about
power and most of us have little say in them, however liberatory their
rhetoric and claimed aims may be. Much of the 20th century was taken
up with combating the destructive effects of such supposedly revolutionary
ideologies. Arguably we are still living with the consequences.

Regaining control of our lives

Most of us know the basics of what we want in our life. Many things
influence these; the times and society we live in; our position in these

133

and our idiosyncratic personal hopes and ambitions. Usually these relate to having health and wellbeing, having love, relationships, friendship and support. We are likely to need paid work for an income, enough to live on and perhaps a bit more, somewhere secure to live and good prospects for our children and grandchildren. These are almost universal aspirations and they are reflected in the constellation of human and civil rights that has emerged and been developed over the years. These include notions of freedom *from* – for example, from want and fear, as well as freedoms *to* – for example, to travel, to have a family life, to justice, to study, to a say in society, and so on.

We know that people who have been disempowered may often have low expectations and limited resources to command what they might hope for. We know that what counts as a decent home and family life will vary at different times, in different societies, with different cultures and according to personal preferences. Nonetheless, we could readily chart what many people want for their lives if we just talked to them.

But this is not generally how the creators of ideology work. Theirs tends to be a back-to-front process instead.

What political ideology is more often about is establishing a set of values and ideas ostensibly about how to achieve what we might want. So, for example, we are told that an unrestricted market is the only way to meet our needs, or that this is only to be achieved by state socialism, or some kind of mixture of the two, or a faith-based state. All these are key current political ideologies globally. None is evidenced to achieve its promise. It's a bit like looking through a telescope from the wrong end. Different ideologies make various claims to secure our hopes and wants, but they don't start with them. They start with their own ideological recipes and commitments, then often say only these will deliver what we want. For me, it feels a bit like saying, the garden will grow better if it is under the market or under the state, rather than, the garden will grow better if the soil is good and we make sure it has the right amount of sun, nutrient and water. Of course the next step is that advocates of each ideology will say that only they can deliver these conditions. Does this remind you of *Animal Farm*? Some ideologies may seem less oppressive than others and some expressions of each may feel preferable. The only thing we can be pretty sure of is that those in charge of each of these systems are likely to feel satisfied by them and to benefit from them. As for the rest of us, as we know, that can be a very different matter.

Ideology can also be like a weather vane telling in which direction to expect its initiators and advocates will try and take us. They won't necessarily tell you that they are committed to values that may well not be in your interests. After all, a sophisticated Right-wing populist tabloid newspaper like the *Daily Mail*, for example, is hardly going to tell its ageing readers that it is committed to low public service spending which leaves them with the threat of unmanageable social care costs and the possible loss of their homes – the inheritance they hoped to pass on to their children. Instead it has tub-thumping campaigns for social care reform, which somehow never seem to sort out the problem!

One lesson highlighted over many years is that only when people can speak for themselves and exert their own power are they likely to be treated with equality. Every step towards real democracy teaches us this. Otherwise without our own voice and power, at worst we can expect to be oppressed and marginalised, at best patronised and sentimentalised. Looking at the portrayal of women, Black people, minority ethnic communities and Indigenous peoples, disabled and LGBTQ people in sexist, racist, disablist, colonialist and heterosexist societies, we may sometimes even wonder which is worse. While exclusionary ideology is often associated with warm and seductive rhetoric, it tends to be guided by the cold logic of the perceived self-interest of those who control it – sometimes as we have seen – dressed up as 'science' to give it more authority.

It has little place for the kindness that can come from the empathy and understanding of being involved in shaping values; of following the golden rule of treating others as you would want to be treated yourself. Recently there has begun to be talk of 'intelligent kindness', in the context of developing and sustaining healthy organisational culture and effective humanistic practice in reaction to the bullying controlling culture created by years of regulatory, structural and managerialist Right-wing ideological reforms (Ballatt et al, 2020). It is not difficult to see how this idea can be extended to challenging top-down controlling ideology through democratising it.

Regaining a say in society

At the same time, political ideology is about much more than what we want for ourselves. It is also about what we want for other people and other groups. It's about how we would want to be treated if we were them or in their situation. Do we believe in and want to see advanced ideals of social justice, treating people with equality and challenging discrimination; valuing diversity and rejecting prejudice and intolerance? Or are we committed to more individualistic, selfish and competitive goals for society? Do we think the first is possible without the second?

This is an age when we know only too well that many politicians seek our support by appealing to our fear and suspicion of the unknown, of foreigners and people who are presented as 'different' or 'other'. We know that there are ideologies which play to such concerns, as well as those which seek to overcome them. We know that the more people are made to feel insecure and disempowered, the more such regressive ideology is likely to flourish. At the same time, we must acknowledge the key issue that all this raises: if we believe in values of inclusivity and equality under the law, then how are these likely to be achieved by ideologies which are developed in the same old exclusionary ways?

Meanwhile, a kind of conjuring trick has been performed – on us all. If we believe what we are told, then we must sign up to whatever ideology seems to promise to deliver our and others' wants and hopes. But these goals and aspirations aren't necessarily the ends of the ideology; those are its commitment to one or other value position. But the reality is the way that they set out to do what they do. As we have said, the promise is that they will deliver what *we* want for us. But it can hardly be said that the Nazis delivered for most Germans or that the Soviet Union did so for most of its populations. In both cases, arbitrary arrest, death and imprisonment ruled and neither regime could be offered as an example of safeguarding personal wellbeing and security. Instead many millions died. At a more banal level, in the UK, Margaret Thatcher promised a 'home-owning democracy' made possible by the market. She sought to achieve this by selling off council housing and encouraging people's borrowing. Now, a generation later, we can see that most of the council housing then sold off has gone to large scale property owners, not owner occupiers and instead of being a nation of owner occupiers as promised, an inadequately regulated private rented sector has massively expanded, offering little security of tenure at disproportionate cost. We are now increasingly a nation of insecure tenants and uncertain tenancies.

Thus massive slippage – between the supposed means of ideologies (market, state, faith, totalitarianism, despotism, and so on) and the rhetorical ends (the promise of a better life for the rest of us) – often ends up resulting in the supposed means (the ideological position) becoming the ends and the pretence that these 'ends' justify the 'means' – often framed in terms of our wellbeing, frequently not achieved.

While we are not saying something crude or simplistic, like 'ideology is bad' or 'all ideologies are the same', what we are suggesting is that if ideologies are narrowly based and controlled by few people, then whatever their progressive rhetoric, they are unlikely ultimately to be empowering for most of us. We are not saying that this is always the case – that there aren't exceptions, or that all ideologies have the same level of participation. Clearly there are differences. But truly participatory ideology seems to be a rarity. It is interesting that one of the most benign and positive externally imposed political ideologies, that which resulted in the creation of the post-war UK welfare state, was subsequently successfully reviled as damaging and paternalistic, to be replaced by a renewed version of the harsh liberal ideology which it had managed to displace (Beresford, 2016).

Critically we argue here that this problem of non-participatory ideology needs to be recognised as an issue; we believe it isn't as yet. Otherwise we will never make progress on it. Then we need to work not only to support ideologies that *express* more liberatory concerns and aims but also those which are emancipatory and participatory in their *process*. We need together to embark on this neglected task of developing ideology together.

Of course, there are strong disincentives against this happening. It is hardly in the interests of existing power holders or of those who seek to take their place. But what can change things is realising there are no short cuts. Other people's causes will never liberate us. We have to build our own. It will not take us very far just crowding behind new, different or rehashed banners. We must build our own causes from the bottom, in the way that every successful move for change has; we must seek to guard ourselves at every stage from the pressures to institutionalisation and autocracy. It's not so much that this struggle must continue. Instead this struggle must actually *start*.

We are clearly now a very long way away from that happening, since developing participatory ideology is still not really even recognised as an issue. Instead the old pattern continues, of counter-ideologies emerging, which tend to be as non-democratic and non-participatory in their process and development as those they ostensibly challenge. It is almost as if regularly we have to go through an endlessly repeating process, of challenging a regressive ideology with a new one making new progressive claims, but with little if any greater involvement, until it takes root and then in turn becomes a further object of our attack as we again realise that it is disempowering and non-participatory, like its predecessor.

This book has focused on ideology imposed on people as something taken for granted, rather than people being able to own it themselves – and on seeking to challenge this. Of course, we may also be accused of having ideological preferences and an ideological position of our own. That is true, but what is different about what we are saying is that people should be enabled to develop and be partners in shaping political ideologies *themselves*. This is still an ideological position, but it is very different to the norm. We are not saying what we want is how it should be. We are saying what people themselves want is how it should be. And we are also making it clear that it must be everybody, not just 'the usual suspects', who have voice, who should be involved; the least powerful as well as the more powerful. And we do not assume that what we want will be what everybody else wants.

What people want changes according to time, place, culture and conditions. We seem currently to be relearning a reality highlighted by Carole Pateman 50 years ago, that citizens marginalised by exclusionary politics need opportunities for involvement. Without these, as we seem to be seeing, they are likely instead to turn to and perpetuate Right-wing populism (Pateman, 1970). But there is a real difference between the often-reactionary demands of manipulated populism and the concerns with equality and social justice that tend to emerge when people have a real chance to work out what they want and to speak for themselves. This is a progressive lesson from history. It is also a lesson of recent years, with the emergence of new social movements: as this process becomes more inclusive, and marginalised and devalued people can make their claim, so demands come more and more to reflect and embrace their rights and needs.

Towards liberatory and sustainable ideology

Much needs to be done to transform our ordinary understanding of and our relationships with ideology. But most of it is far from 'rocket science' and there is already much learning from related fields to draw on. There are a few key steps that will get us onto this different participatory road.

- First, we have to recognise there is an issue here to be dealt with. What is most needed to reclaim ideology is to start the journey of recognising the need to do so.
- The next key step is to support and encourage accessible discussions about ideology that take account of the reality that the term has little meaning for most people.
- Then much needs to be done to address participation in relation to the formulation of ideology. But we already know a lot about how to do this.
- We will need to get together to explore participatory ideology. It is a task that demands collective action as well as individual commitment.

- It also requires capacity building and support for empowerment, if we are all to be effective participants in ideology for positive change, rather than the usual stage army.
- Finally, by involvement we must mean seeking inclusive and diverse involvement drawing on the significant amount of experience already available to challenge existing barriers and exclusions.

At a time when the very future of the planet is uncertain and conflict both within societies and between them seems to be at a high, we urgently need some kind of seismic change that prioritises personal, collective and global security and wellbeing. Widespread recognition of the UK prime minister Boris Johnson administration's inadequate response to the COVID-19 pandemic and the defeat of Donald Trump in the 2020 US presidential elections may signify the first glimmerings of such change. But one of the lessons for me of writing this book is that, when it comes to ideology (and indeed many other important issues affecting our lives), we can really only do it for ourselves. At the time of writing this is most powerfully being demonstrated by the Black Lives Matter and #MeToo movements and growing popular pressure to do more to halt destructive climate change. There is no ideology from other people that will work to free or save us. We have to be involved in developing our own. There may be better and worse ideologies, but the only truly sustainable and liberatory ideology is the ideology that we own. That such an overarching aspect of all our lives should largely be beyond our control is to say the least alarming. It is especially alarming at times like the present when global security is so uncertain and the very future of the planet so much in question. As yet this issue of the ownership of ideology doesn't even seem to be on any major political or even grassroots agenda. This must change. Hopefully the discussion that has been initiated here will help begin to make this possible for more and more groups and more and more people in more and more places.

References

Adams, T. (2009), 'Margaret Atwood on a Voyage to the World's End', *The Observer*, 29 August, www.theguardian.com/theobserver/2009/aug/30/margaret-atwood-novel-ecology, accessed 9 September 2020.

Adorno, T.W., Frenkel-Brunswik, E., Levinson, D.J. and Sanford, R.N. (1950), *The Authoritarian Personality*, New York, Harper and Row.

Alinsky, S.D. (1971), *Rules for Radicals: A Pragmatic Primer for Realistic Radicals*, New York, Random House Publishing.

Another Bleedin Monty Python Website (undated), '*Life of Brian* Script: Scene 8: The Grumpy People's Front Of Judea, *Life of Brian*, Scene Eight', http://montypython.50webs.com/scripts/Life_of_Brian/8.htm, accessed 28 March 2020.

Arches, J. and Fleming, J. (2006), 'Young people and social action: youth participation in the UK and USA', *New Directions for Youth Development*, Vol 111, Fall, pp 89–91.

Arendt, H. (1951), *The Origins of Totalitarianism*, second edition, New York, Meridian Books.

Arnstein, S. (1969), 'A ladder of citizen participation', *Journal of the American Planning Association*, Vol 35, No 4, pp 216–24.

Ashford, D.E. (1972), *Ideology and Participation*, California, Sage Publications.

Atkinson, M. (1984), *Our Masters' Voices: The Language and Body Language of Politics*, London, Routledge.

Ballatt, J., Campling, P. and Maloney, C. (2020), *Intelligent Kindness: Rehabilitating the Welfare State,* second edition, Cambridge, Cambridge University Press in association with the Royal College of Psychiatry.

Barnett-Cormack, S. (2018), 'Grassroots tackling policy: the making of the Spartacus report', in Beresford, P. and Carr, S. (editors), *Social Policy First Hand: An International Introduction to Participatory Social Welfare*, Bristol, Policy Press, pp 355–61.

Beevor, A. (2006), *The Battle for Spain: The Spanish Civil War 1936–1939*, London, Penguin Books.

Bell, B., Gaventa, J. and Peters, J. (editors) (1990), *We Make the Road by Walking: Conversations on Education and Social Change, Myles Horton and Paulo Freire*, Philadelphia, Temple University Press.

Beresford, P. (1979) 'The public presentation of vagrancy', in Cook, T. (editor), *Vagrancy: Some New Perspectives*, London, Academic Press, pp 141–65.

Beresford, P. (2003), *It's Our Lives: A Short Theory of Knowledge, Distance and Experience*, London, Citizen Press in association with Shaping Our Lives.

Beresford, P. (2010), *A Straight Talking Guide to Being a Mental Health Service User*, Ross-on-Wye, PCCS Books.

Beresford, P. (2012), From 'vulnerable' to vanguard: challenging the Coalition', *Soundings: A Journal of Politics and Culture*, Vol 50, Spring, pp 46–57.

Beresford, P. (2013), *Beyond the Usual Suspects: Towards Inclusive User Involvement – Research Report*, London, Shaping Our Lives.

Beresford, P. (2016), *All Our Welfare: Towards Participatory Social Policy*, Bristol, Policy Press.

Beresford, P. (2018), 'A failure of national mental health policy and the failure of a global summit, comment', *British Journal of Mental Health Nursing*, November, Vol 7, No 5, pp 198–9.

Beresford, P. (2019a), 'Public participation in health and social care: exploring the co-production of knowledge', *Frontiers in Sociology, Medical Sociology*, 4 January, www.frontiersin.org/articles/10.3389/fsoc.2018.00041/full

Beresford, P. (2019b), 'Rethinking 1980's social policy: the struggle from powerlessness to participation', *Society, Back to the Future: 1979–1989*, National Library of Scotland, https://digital.nls.uk/1980s/society/social-policy/, accessed 2 April 2020.

Beresford, P. (2020), 'The psychiatrisation of politics: reasons to be very afraid', *Asylum*, Vol 27, No 1, Spring, pp 23–4.

Beresford, P. and Beresford, S. (1978), *A Say in the Future: Planning, Participation and Meeting Social Need*, London, Battersea Community Action.

Beresford, P. and Branfield, F. (2012), 'Building solidarity, ensuring diversity: lessons from service users' and disabled people's movements', in Barnes, M. and Cotterell, P. (editors) *Critical Perspectives on User Involvement*, Bristol, Policy Press, pp 33–45.

Beresford, P. and Carr, S. (editors) (2018), *Social Policy First Hand: An International Introduction to Participatory Social Policy*, Bristol, Policy Press.

Beresford, P. and Croft, S. (1986), *Whose Welfare: Private Care or Public Services?*, Brighton, Lewis Cohen Urban Studies Centre at University of Brighton.

Beresford, P. and Croft, S. (1988), 'Being on the receiving end – lessons for community development and user involvement', *Community Development Journal*, Vol 23, No 4, October, pp 273–9.

Beresford, P. and Croft, S. (1993a), *Citizen Involvement: A Practical Guide for Change*, Basingstoke, Macmillan.

Beresford, P. and Croft, S. (1993b), *Getting Involved: A Practical Manual*, London, Joseph Rowntree Foundation and Open Services Project.

Beresford, P., Fleming, J., Glynn, M., Bewley, C., Croft, S., Branfield, F. and Postle, K. (2011), *Supporting People: Towards a Person-Centred Approach*, Bristol, Policy Press.

Berman, M. (2001), *The Twilight of American Culture*, London, W.W. Norton.

Blumental, D.S. (2011), 'Is community-based participatory research possible?', *American Journal of Preventive Medicine*, Vol 40, No 3, March, pp 386–9.

Bonaparte, N. (undated), BrainyQuote, www.brainyquote.com/quotes/napoleon_bonaparte_383308, accessed 28 March 2020.

Brosnan, L. (2018), 'Who's talking about us without us? A survivor research interjection into an academic psychiatry debate on compulsory community treatment orders in Ireland', *Laws*, Vol 7, No 4, pp 33–48.

Brown, D.L. (2020), ' "It was a modern-day lynching" ': violent deaths reflect a brutal American legacy', 5 June, *National Geographic*, www.nationalgeographic.co.uk/history-and-civilisation/2020/06/it-was-a-modern-day-lynching-violent-deaths-reflect-a-brutal, accessed 29 July 2020.

Buechler, S.M. (1999), *Social Movements in Advanced Capitalism*, Oxford, Oxford University Press.

Burns, J.H. and Hart, H.A.R. (editors) (1977), 'A comment on The Commentaries and a fragment on government', in *The Collected Works of Jeremy Bentham*, London, University College London.

Campbell, J. and Oliver, M. (1996), *Disability Politics: Understanding Our Past, Changing Our Future*, London, Routledge.

Camus, A. (2000), *The Rebel*, London, Penguin Books.

Carr, S. (2019), 'I am not your nutter: a personal reflection on commodification and comradeship in service user and survivor research', *Disability and Society*, Vol 34, No 7–8, pp 1140–53.

Cheng, Y.C. (2012), *School Effectiveness and School-Based Management: A Mechanism for Development*, London, Routledge.

Chomsky, N. (2015), *On Power and Ideology*, Chomsky.info, https://chomsky.info/on-power-and-ideology/, accessed 16 March 2020.

Coaston, J. (2019), 'The intersectionality wars', The Highlight, *Vox*, www.vox.com/the-highlight/2019/5/20/18542843/intersectionality-conservatism-law-race-gender-discrimination, accessed 9 April 2020.

Cobb, R.W. (1973), 'Review of Ashford, D.E. (1972), *Ideology and Participation*', *American Political Science Review*, Vol 71, No 3, pp 1121–2.

Coleridge, P. (1993), *Disability, Liberation And Development*, Oxford, Oxfam in association with Action on Disability and Development.

Collins, K. and Ison, R. (2006), 'Dare we jump off Arnstein's ladder? Social learning as a new policy paradigm', in *Proceedings of PATH (Participatory Approaches in Science and Technology) Conference*, 4–7 June, Edinburgh, Open Research online, http://oro.open.ac.uk/8589/1/Path_paper_Collins_Ison.pdf

Cooke, B. and Kothari, U. (editors) (2001) *Participation: The New Tyranny?*, London, Zed Books.

Cowper, A. (2020), 'Ambitious rhetoric and appalling reality: The UK government's response to COVID-19', *British Medical Journal*, Vol 369.

Croteau, D.R. and Hoynes, W.D. (2018), *Media/Society: Technology, Industries, Content and Users*, sixth edition, London, Sage.

Cusack, J. (undated), AllGreatQuotes, www.allgreatquotes.com/quote-202186/, accessed 2 April 2020.

Davis, A. (2018), 'Open future', *The Economist*, 3 July, www.economist.com/open-future/2018/07/03/the-gender-identity-movement-undermines-lesbians, accessed 30 March 2020.

Day, E. (2015), '#BlackLivesMatter: the birth of a new civil rights movement', *Observer*, 19 July, www.theguardian.com/world/2015/jul/19/blacklivesmatter-birth-civil-rights-movement, accessed 28 July 2020.

de St Aubin, E. (1996), 'Personal ideology polarity: its emotional foundation and its manifestation in individual value systems, religiosity, political orientation, and assumptions concerning human nature', *Journal of Personal Social Psychology*, July, No 1, Vol 71, pp 152–65.

Dorling, D. (2015), *Inequality and the 1%*, London, Verso Books.

Eagleton, T. (1991), *Ideology: An Introduction*, London, Verso.

Eagleton, T. (1994), *Ideology*, London, Longman.

Eagleton, T. (2007), *Ideology: An Introduction*, second edition, London, Verso.

Einstein, A. (undated) Albert Einstein, BrainyQuote, www.brainyquote.com/quotes/albert_einstein_148778, accessed 10 April, 2020.

Eliot, T.S. (2001), *Four Quartets*, London, Faber.

Fairclough, N. (2000), *New Labour, New Language*, London, Routledge.

Fanon, F. (1967 [1952]), *Black Skin, White Masks*, translation by Charles Lam Markmann, New York, Grove Press.

Feldman, S. and Johnston, C. (2013), 'Understanding the determinants of political ideology: implications of structural complexity', *Political Psychology*, Vol 35, No 3, Wiley online library, https://scholar.google.co.uk/scholar?q=Understanding+the+Determinants+of+Political+Ideology:+Implications+of+Structural+Complexity+Stanley+Feldman++Christopher+Johnston&hl=en&as_sdt=0&as_vis=1&oi=scholart, accessed 24 March 2020.

Feuer, L.S. (2017), *Ideology and the Ideologists*, Abingdon, Routledge.

Fileborn, B. and Loney-Howes, R. (editors) (2019), *#MeToo and the Politics of Social Change*, Basingstoke, Palgrave Macmillan.

Filipovic, J. (2019), 'Death sentence for abortion? The hypocrisy of US "pro-lifers" is plain to see', *The Guardian*, 11 April, www.theguardian.com/commentisfree/2019/apr/11/death-sentence-abortion-hypocrisy-pro-life, accessed 20 March 2020.

Findley, T. (1972), 'Huey Newton: twenty-five floors from the street: "I lost my capacity to hate. I just disagree"', *Rolling Stone*, 3 August, www.rollingstone.com/culture/culture-news/huey-newton-twenty-five-floors-from-the-street-176820/, accessed 7 April 2020.

Fleming, J. and Ward, D. (2004), 'Methodology and practical application of the social action research model', in Maggs-Rapport, F. (editor) *New Qualitative Research Methodologies in Health and Social Care*, London, Routledge.

Foucault, M. (1988), *Madness And Civilisation: A History of Insanity in the Age of Reason*, New York, Vintage.

Franks, B. (2013), 'Anarchism', in Freeden, M. and Stears, M. (editors) *The Oxford Handbook of Political Ideologies*, Oxford, Oxford University Press, pp 385–404.

Freeden, M. (1996), *Ideologies and Political Theory: A Conceptual Approach*, Oxford, Clarendon Press.

Freeden, M. (2006), 'Ideology and political theory', *Journal of Political Ideologies*, Vol 11, No 1, pp 3–22.

Freeden, M., Sargent, L.T. and Stears, M. (editors) (2013), *The Oxford Handbook of Political Ideologies*, Oxford, Oxford University Press.

Freeman, J. (1972–73), 'The tyranny of structurelessness', *Berkeley Journal of Sociology*, No 17, pp 151–64.

Freeman, M. (2003), *Ideology: A Very Short Introduction*, Oxford, Oxford University Press.

Frega, R. (2013), 'The epistemology of resistance, book review', *European Journal of Pragmatism and American Philosophy*, Vol 1, https://journals.openedition.org/ejpap/678, accessed 15 April 2019.

Freire, P. (1972), *Pedagogy of the Oppressed*, London, Penguin.

Fricker, M. (2007), *Epistemic Injustice: Power and the Ethics of Knowing*, Oxford, Oxford University Press.

Fritzsche, P. (1990), *Rehearsals for Fascism: Populism and Political Mobilization in Weimar Germany*, New York, Oxford University Press.

Fukuyama, F. (1989). 'The end of history?', *The National Interest*, Vol 16, pp 3–18.

Fukuyama, F. (1992), *The End of History and The Last Man*, New York, Free Press.

Gandhi, M. (undated), BrainyQuote, www.brainyquote.com/quotes/mahatma_gandhi_163698, accessed 2 November 2020.

Gaventa, J. (1982), *Power and Powerlessness: Quiescence and Rebellion in an Appalachian Valley*, Chicago, University of Illinois Press.

Ghaderinezhad, B. (2015), 'On the relationship between language and ideology represented in CDA texts', *International Journal of Humanities and Cultural Studies*, Special Issue, December, pp 878–89.

Gibson, M.R. (2013), 'The "anarchism" of the Occupy Movement', *Australian Journal of Political Science*, Vol 48, No 3, pp 335–48.

Giddens, A. and Sutton, P.W. (editors) (2017), *Sociology*, eighth edition, Cambridge, Polity Press.

Gramsci, A. (1971), *Selections from The Prison Notebooks*, New York, International Publishers.

Habermas, J. (1971), *Towards a Rational Society: Student Protest, Science and Politics*, Boston, Beacon Press.

Hall, B.L. (2011), 'Towards a knowledge democracy movement: contemporary trends in community-university research partnerships', *Rizoma freireano, Rhizome freirean*, Vol 9, Spain, Instituto Paulo Freire de Espagna.

Haralambos, M. and Holborn, M. (editors) (2008), *Sociology: Themes and Perspectives*, seventh edition, London, Collins Educational.

Harding, N. (1996), *Leninism*, Basingstoke, Macmillan.

Harrison, K. and Boyd, T. (2003), *Understanding Political Ideas and Movements*, Manchester, Manchester University Press.

Hawkes, D. (2003), *Ideology: The New Critical Idiom*, second edition, London, Routledge.

Heller, N. (2017), 'Is there any point to protesting? Critic at large', *The New Yorker*, 21 August, www.newyorker.com/magazine/2017/08/21/is-there-any-point-to-protesting, accessed 5 April 2020.

Heywood, A. (2013), *Politics*, fourth edition, Basingstoke, Palgrave.

Heywood, A. (2017), *Political Ideologies: An Introduction*, sixth edition, London, Red Globe Press.

Hickey, S.S. and Mohan, S.G. (editors) (2004), *Participation – From Tyranny to Transformation: Exploring New Approaches to Participation in Development*, London, Zed Books.

Hill, C. (1940), *The English Revolution 1640*, London, Lawrence and Wishart.

Hill Collins, P. and Bilge, S. (2016), *Intersectionality*, Key Concepts, London, Wiley.

Hillstrom, L.C. (2019), *The #MeToo Movement*, first edition, California, ABC-CLIO.

Hoban, M., James, V., Beresford, P. and Fleming, J. (2013) *Shaping Our Age – Involving Older Age: The Route to Twenty First Century Well-Being. Final Report*, Cardiff, Royal Voluntary Service.

Hobbes, T. (2016), *Leviathan*, London, Penguin Classics.

Hoffman, J. and Graham, P. (2006), *Introduction to Political Ideologies*, London, Pearson Education.

Hoggett, P. and Bishop, J. (1986), *Organising around Enthusiasms: Patterns of Mutual Aid in Leisure*, London, Comedia.

Honderich, T. (1995), *The Oxford Companion to Philosophy*, Oxford, Oxford University Press.

hooks, b. (1984), *Feminist Theory: From Margin to Center*, Boston, South End Press.

Horner, J. (2018), 'Police killings of 3 black men left a mark on Detroit's history more than 50 years ago', *The Conversation*, 10 September, https://theconversation.com/police-killings-of-3-black-men-left-a-mark-on-detroits-history-more-than-50-years-ago-101716, accessed 29 July 2020.

Huemer, M. (2012), *The Problem of Political Authority: An Examination of the Right to Coerce and the Duty to Obey*, Basingstoke, Palgrave Macmillan.

Humphrey, M. and Umbach, M. (undated), *The Concept of Ideology in Policy and Politics*, video interview, Nottingham, University of Nottingham, FutureLearn, www.futurelearn.com/courses/propaganda/0/steps/25103, accessed 9 March 2020.

Hunt, J. (2019), *No Limits: The Disabled People's Movement – A Radical History*, London, TBR Consulting.

Hunt, P. (1981), 'Settling accounts with the parasite people: a critique of *A Life Apart* by E.J. Miller and G.V. Gwynne', *Disability Challenge*, No 1, pp 37–50.

Jackson Lears, T.J. (1985), 'The concept of cultural hegemony: problems and possibilities', *American Historical Review*, Vol 90, No 3, June, pp 567–93.

Jordan, T. and Lent, A (editors) (1999), *Storming the Millennium: The New Politics of Change*, London, Lawrence and Wishart.

Josephson, P.R. (2005), *Totalitarian Science and Technology*, second edition, New York, Humanity Books.

Jost, J.T., Ledgerwood, A. and Hardin, C.D. (2008), 'Shared reality, system justification, and the relational basis of ideological beliefs', *Social and Personality Psychology Compass*, No 2, pp 171–86.

Kara, H. (2017), 'Identity and power in co-produced activist research', *Qualitative Research*, Vol 17, No 3, pp 289–301.

Karabel, J. and Halsey, A.H. (editors) (1977), *Power and Ideology in Education*, Oxford, Oxford University Press.

Kennedy, E. (1979), '"Ideology": from Destutt De Tracy to Marx', *Journal of the History of Ideas*, July–September, Vol 40, No 3, pp 353–68.

Kennedy, L. (1992), *Business Etiquette for the Nineties: Your Ticket to Career Success*, North Charleston, Palmetto Publishers, p 8.

Kershaw, I. (1987), *The Hitler Myth: Image and Reality in the Third Reich*, Oxford, Oxford University Press.

Koestler, A. (1980), *Darkness at Noon*, London, Folio Society.

Kropotkin, P. (2020), *Anarchist Communism*, London, Penguin Books.

Kuhn, T.S. (1970), *The Structure of Scientific Revolution*, second edition, Berkeley, University of California Press.

Kumar, K. (2006), 'Ideology and sociology: reflections on Karl Mannheim's *Ideology and Utopia*', *Journal of Political Ideologies*, Vol 11, No 2, pp 169–81.

Le Grand, J. (1997), 'Knights, knaves or pawns? Human behaviour and social policy', *Journal of Social Policy*, Vol 26, No 2, pp 149–69.

Leach, R. (2015), *Political Ideology in Britain*, third edition, Basingstoke, Palgrave.

LeFrancois, B.A., Menzies, R., Reaume, G. (eds) (2013), *Mad Matters: A Critical Reader in Canadian Mad Studies*, Toronto, Canadian Scholars Press.

Lent, A. (2002), *British Social Movements since 1945: Sex, Colour, Peace and Power*, Basingstoke: Macmillan/Palgrave.

Li, C. (2020), 'Confronting history: James Baldwin', *Kinfolk*, Vol 37, www.kinfolk.com/confronting-history-james-baldwin/, accessed 16 October 2020.

Lister, R. (1991), 'Citizenship engendered', *Critical Social Policy*, Vol 11, No 32, pp 65–71.

Lister, R. (2003), *Citizenship: Feminist Perspectives*, second edition, London, Palgrave.

Lloyd, M. (2005), *Beyond Identity Politics: Feminism, Power and Politics*, London, Sage.

Lorde, A. (1984), *Sister Outsider*, Berkeley, Ten Speed Press.

Lorde, A. (2007), 'The master's tools will never dismantle the master's house (1984)', *Sister Outsider: Essays and Speeches*, Berkeley, CA, Crossing Press, pp 110–14.

Lukes, S. (2004), *Power: A Radical View*, second edition, Basingstoke, Palgrave Macmillan.

Lynch, W.T. (1994), 'Ideology and the sociology of scientific knowledge', *Social Studies of Science*, Vol 24, No 2, May, pp 197–227.

Macionis, J.J. (2010), *Sociology*, thirteenth edition, Hoboken, Pearson Education.

Mackay, M. (2016), 'Making sense of critical participatory action research. Reflections on the Action Research Planner: doing critical participatory action research', *International Practice Development Journal*, Vol 6, No 2, pp 1–3.

Madden, M. and Speed, E. (2017), 'Beware zombies and unicorns: toward critical patient and public involvement in health research in a neoliberal context', *Frontiers in Sociology*, Vol 2, No 7, doi: 10.3389/soc.2017.00007

Marshall, P.H. (1993), *Demanding the Impossible: A History of Anarchism*, London, Fontana.

Martin, W.P. (2004), *The Best Liberal Quotes Ever: Why the Left Is Right*, Chicago, Source Books, p 173.

McLennan, D. (1986), *Ideology*, Minnesota, University of Minnesota.

Medina, J. (2012), *The Epistemology of Resistance*, Oxford, Oxford University Press.

Menand, L. (2018), 'Francis Fukuyama postpones the end of history', *The New Yorker*, 27 August, www.newyorker.com/magazine/2018/09/03/francis-fukuyama-postpones-the-end-of-history, accessed 12 March 2020.

Miller, W. (1936), *I Found No Peace: The Journal of a Foreign Correspondent*, New York, The Literary Guild.

Mills, C.W. (1959), *The Sociological Imagination*, Oxford, Oxford University Press.

Morris, J. (1993), *Independent Lives? Community Care and Disabled People*, Basingstoke, Macmillan.

Morris, J. (editor) (1996), *Encounters with Strangers: Feminism and Disability*, London, The Women's Press.

Morris, M. (2016), *Knowledge and Ideology: The Epistemology of Social and Political Critique*, Cambridge, Cambridge University Press.

Mount, F. (2012), 'The end of ideology again? Essay', *Public Policy Research*, Institute for Public Policy Research, Vol 19, No 2, pp 112–18.

Moynihan, D.P. (undated) BrainyQuote, www.brainyquote.com/quotes/daniel_patrick_moynihan_116275, accessed 30 March 2020.

Needham, C. and Carr, S. (2009), 'Co-production: an emerging evidence base for adult social care transformation', *SCIE Research Briefing* 31, June, London, Social Care Institute for Excellence.

Oliver, K. Kothari, A. and Mays, N. (2019), 'The dark side of coproduction: do the costs outweigh the benefits for health research?', *Health Research Policy and Systems*, 28 March, Vol 17, No 33, https://health-policy-systems.biomedcentral.com/articles/10.1186/s12961-019-0432-3, accessed 3 August 2020.

Oliver, M. (1983), *Social Work and Disabled People*, Basingstoke, Macmillan.

Oliver, M. (1990), *The Politics of Disablement*, Basingstoke, Macmillan Education.

Oliver, M. (1996), *Understanding Disability: From Theory to Practice*, Basingstoke, Macmillan.

Oliver, M. (2009), *Understanding Disability: From Theory to Practice*, second edition, Basingstoke, Palgrave Macmillan.

Oliver, M. and Barnes, C. (1998), *Disabled People and Social Policy: From Exclusion to Inclusion*, London, Longman.

Oliver, M. and Barnes, C. (2012), *The New Politics of Disablement*, Basingstoke, Palgrave Macmillan.

Orwell, G. (1938), *Homage to Catalonia*, London, Secker and Warburg.

Orwell, G. (1945) *Animal Farm: A Fairy Story*, London, Secker and Warburg.

Orwell, G. (1949), *Nineteen Eighty-Four*, London, Penguin.

Orwell, G. (2013 [1946]), *Politics and the English Language*, London, Penguin.

Pateman, C. (1970), *Participation and Democratic Theory*, Cambridge, Cambridge University Press.

Perraudin, F. (2015), 'Jeremy Corbyn suggests he would bring back Labour's nationalising clause IV', *The Guardian*, 9 August, www.theguardian.com/politics/2015/aug/08/jeremy-corbyn-could-bring-back-labours-clause-iv-on-public-ownership, accessed 29 March 2020.

Petcoff, A. (2017), 'The problem with Saul Alinsky', 5 October, *Jacobin Magazine*, https://jacobinmag.com/2017/05/saul-alinsky-alinskyism-organizing-methods-cesar-chavez-ufw, accessed 1 April 2020.

Philo, G. Briant, E. and Donald, P. (2013), *Bad News for Refugees*, London, Pluto Press.

Philosiblog (2013), *Quoting Marie Curie*, https://philosiblog.com/2013/11/07/we-must-believe-that-we-are-gifted-for-something-and-that-this-thing-must-be-attained/, accessed 9 September 2020.

Raaflaub, K.A. (2007), 'The breakthrough of *demokratia* in mid-fifth-century Athens', in Raaflaub, K.A., Ober, J. and Wallace, R. (editors) *Origins of Democracy in Ancient Greece*, Berkeley, University of California Press.

Ragavan, I. (2000), *The Moral and Political Thought of Mahatma Gandhi*, Uttar Pradesh, Oxford University Press India.

Riley, B. (undated), BrainyQuote, www.brainyquote.com/quotes/boots_riley_931472, accessed 6 April 2020.

Ritzer, G. (2008), *The McDonaldization of Society*, Los Angeles, Pine Forest Press.

Rose, D., Carr, S. and Beresford, P. (2018), 'Widening cross-disciplinary research for mental health: What is missing from the Research Councils UK', *Disability and Society*, Vol 33, No 3, pp 476–81.

Ross, L.F., Loup, A., Nelson, R.M., Botkin, J.R., Kost, R., Smith, G.R. and Gehlert, S. (2010), 'The challenges of collaboration for academic and community partners in a research partnership: points to consider', *Journal of Empirical Research and Human Research Ethics*, Vol 5, No 1, pp 19–31.

Rowbotham, S. (1973), *Hidden from History: 300 Years of Women's Oppression and the Fight against It*, London, Pluto Press.

Rowbotham, S. (1989), *The Past Is Before Us: Feminism in Action since the 1960s*, London, HarperCollins.

Rowbotham, S., Segal, L. and Wainwright, H. (1979), *Beyond the Fragments: Feminism and the Making of Socialism*, London, Merlin Press.

Rowbotham, S., Segal, L. and Wainwright, H. (2013), *Beyond the Fragments: Feminism and the Making of Socialism*, Third Edition, London, Merlin Press.

Rowell, L. and Feldman, A. (2019), 'Knowledge democracy and action research, editorial', Special Issue, Knowledge Democracy, Educational Action Research, 3 February, Vol 27, No 1, pp 1–6.

Russell, J. (2005), 'New Labour has nurtured this selfish individualism, Politics', *The Guardian*, 28 May, www.theguardian.com/politics/2005/may/28/labour.uk, accessed 12 March 2020.

Russo, J., Beresford, P. and O'Hagan, M. (2018), 'Commentary on Happell, B. and Scholz, B. *Doing What We Can, But Knowing Our Place: Being an Ally to Promote Consumer Leadership in Mental Health*', *International Journal of Mental Health Nursing*, No 27, pp 440–7.

Rustin, B. (1969), 'To the children of Cleveland December 3rd 1969, after a city leader had invited him to write a letter for public exhibit to help children understand "the magnificent times in which we live"', cited in Huffpost, Bayard Rustin in His Own Words, 'I must resist', 15 March 2013, www.huffpost.com/entry/bayard-rustin-in-his-own_b_2881057?guccounter=1&guce_referrer=aHR0cHM6Ly93d3cuZ29vZ2xlLmNvLnVrLw&guce_referrer_sig=AQAAAEftifslj18fPKadJ60vTkAmUUaysJRbsFTEr_BmslMGisTlhKRdgEhrOKJFz55rCR7KBBLIuUwc412PZSKnkzpKkZeGU3tAXcqnpkXhU4H97gA17hVWF5G2sbqIQz1AVR1hxjTe6XzNtOd5GdFn80fMLXrxggFb0NqJAgfZUclr , accessed 28 March 2020.

Ryan, F. (2019), *Crippled: Austerity and the Demonization of Disabled People*, London, Verso.

Saad-Filho, A. (2020), From COVID-19 to the end of neoliberalism, *Critical Sociology*, 29 May, https://doi.org/10.1177/0896920520929966, accessed 16 October 2020.

Safransky, S. (1990), *Sunbeams: A Book of Quotations*, US, North Atlantic Books.

Savage, M. (2020), 'More than half of England's coronavirus-related deaths will be people from care homes', *The Guardian*, 7 June, www.theguardian.com/society/2020/jun/07/more-than-half-of-englands-coronavirus-related-deaths-will-be-people-from-care-homes, accessed 29 July 2020.

Seliger, M. (1976), *Ideology and Politics*, London, Allen and Unwin.

Shakespeare, T. (2014), *Disability Rights and Wrongs Revisited*, second edition, Abingdon, Routledge.

Shakespeare, T. (2017), *Disability: The Basics*, London, Routledge

Shakespeare, T., Gillespie-Sells, K. and Davies, D. (1997), *The Sexual Politics of Disability: Untold Desires*, London, Cassell.

Shera, W. and Wells, L.M. (editors) (1999), *Empowerment Practice in Social Work: Developing Richer Conceptual Foundations*, Toronto: Canadian Scholars' Press.

Shorten, A. (2015), *Contemporary Political Theory*, London, Red Globe Press.

Shriver, M. (2011), Gloria Steinem, Interview, 11 July, *Interview Magazine*, www.interviewmagazine.com/culture/gloria-steinem, accessed 6 April 2020.

Simmons, R. Powell, M. and Greener, I. (editors) (2009), *The Consumer in Public Services: Choice, Values and Difference*, Bristol, Policy Press.

Smale, G. (1998), *Social Work and Social Problems: Working towards Social Inclusion*, London, National Institute for Social Work.

Smith, P.A. (1989), *On Political War*, Washington, National Defense University Press.

Stalin, J. (undated), Goodreads quote, www.goodreads.com/quotes/ 7597980-it-is-difficult-for-me-to-imagine-what-personal-liberty, accessed 24 March 2020.

Standing, G. (2015), 'Magna Carta: 800 years on we need a new people's charter', *The Guardian*, 23 January, www.theguardian.com/ commentisfree/2015/jan/23/magna-carta-new-peoples-charter, accessed 7 April 2020.

Statista Research Department (2020), 'People shot to death by US police 2017–2020 by race', 31 July, *Statista Research Department*, www. statista.com/statistics/585152/people-shot-to-death-by-us-police- by-race/, accessed 3 August 2020.

Steinem, G. (2012), *Outrageous Acts and Everyday Rebellions*, second edition, New York, Open Road Media.

Stevenson, O. and Parsloe, P. (1993), *Community Care and Empowerment*, York, Joseph Rowntree Foundation.

Stewart, M. (2016), *Cash Not Care: The Planned Demolition of the Welfare State*, London, New Generation.

Street, J., Duszynski, K., Krawczk, S. and Braunack-Mayer, A. (2014), 'The use of citizens' juries in health policy decision-making: a systematic review', *Social Science and Medicine*, Vol 109, May, pp 1–9.

Tawney, R.H. (2016 [1922]), *Religion and the Rise of Capitalism*, London, Verso.

Telegraph View (2015), 'The disturbing roots of Corbynism exposed', *Daily Telegraph*, 27 September, www.telegraph.co.uk/comment/ telegraph-view/11893307/The-disturbing-roots-of-Corbynism- exposed.html, accessed 11 March 2020.

Therborn, G. (1999), *The Ideology of Power and the Power of Ideology*, new edition, London, Verso.

Thomas, C. (2007), *Sociologies of Disability and Illness: Contested Ideas in Disability Studies and Medical Sociology*, Basingstoke, Palgrave Macmillan.

Thompson, J.B. (1984), *Studies in the Theory of Ideology*, Berkeley, University of California.

Thompson, N. (2016), *Culture as Weapon*, New York, Melville House Publishing.

Thorley, J. (2005), *Athenian Democracy*, London, Routledge.

Tooze, A. (2006), *The Wages of Destruction: The Making and Breaking of the Nazi Economy*, New York, Penguin.

Touraine, A. (1981), *The Voice and the Eye: An Analysis of Social Movements*, Cambridge, Cambridge University Press.

Tressell, R. (2004), *The Ragged Trousered Philanthropists*, London, Penguin Books.

Turner, M. and Beresford, P. (2005), *User Controlled Research: Its Meanings and Potential, Final Report*, Shaping Our Lives and the Centre for Citizen Participation, Brunel University, Eastleigh, Involve.

UPIAS (Union of the Physically Impaired Against Segregation) and Disability Alliance (1976), 'Fundamental principles of disability: being a summary of the discussion held on 22nd November, 1975 and containing commentaries from each organization', London, Union of the Physically Impaired Against Segregation and the Disability Alliance.

Vago, S. (2019), *Social Change*, fifth edition, London, Pearson.

van Dijk, T.A. (2006), *Politics, Ideology and Discourse, Politics of Teaching*, pp 729–38, doi: 10.1016/B0-08-044854-2/00722-7

Walker, A. (undated), BrainyQuote, www.brainyquote.com/quotes/alice_walker_625860, accessed 28 October 2020.

Watzlawick, P., Weakland, J. and Fisch, R. (1974), *Change: Principles of Problem Formation and Problem Resolution*, New York, W.W. Norton and Co.

Wetherly, P. (2017), *Political Ideologies*, Oxford, Oxford University Press.

Williams O., Sarre, S., Papoulias, S.C., Knowles, S., Robert, G., Beresford, P., Rose, D., Carr, S., Kaur, M., and Palmer, V.J. (2020), 'Lost in the shadows: reflections on the dark side of co-production', *Health Research Policy and Systems*, Vol 18, No 43.

Winkler, F. (1987), 'Consumerism in health care: beyond the supermarket model', *Policy and Politics*, Vol 15, No 1, January, pp 1–8.

Wittgenstein, L. (2013), *Tractatus-Logico-Philosophicus*, translated by Pears, D. and McGuinness, B., London, Routledge.

Wodak, R. (2015), *The Politics of Fear: What Right-Wing Populist Discourses Mean*, London, Sage.

Woodward, B. (2018), *Fear: Trump in the White House*, New York, Simon and Schuster.

Young, S. (undated), BrainyQuote, www.brainyquote.com/quotes/stella_young_693424, accessed 3 April 2020.

Yuval-Davis, N. (2006), 'Intersectionality and feminist politics', *European Journal of Women's Studies*, 1 August, Vol 13, No 3, pp 103–209.

Zaidi, A. (2012), 'Language of ideology/ideology of language: notes on theory and practice', *Journal of Postcolonial Cultures and Societies*, Vol 3, No 1, pp 71–88.

Index